SUICIDE
Volume 2

A collection of poetry, short prose, interviews and personal stories from around the world on the themes of suicide and self-harm.

Compiled by Robin Barratt

SUICIDE
Volume 2

ISBN: 9798388770455
© Robin Barratt and all the authors herein, April, 2023

All rights reserved. No part of this publication may be reproduced, distributed, or transmitted in any form or by any means, including photocopying, recording, or other electronic or mechanical methods, without the prior written permission of the publisher, except in the case of brief quotations embodied in critical reviews and certain other non-commercial uses permitted by copyright law. For permission requests, contact the publisher at the address below.

Published independently by Robin Barratt
www.RobinBarratt.co.uk

Illustrations by Daniella Barratt

TRIGGER WARNING!

This book contains poetry and interviews about trauma, personality disorders, suicidal thoughts, self-harming, depression and other significant mental health issues.

Survivors of Bereavement by Suicide

The Survivors of Bereavement by Suicide exists to meet the needs and break the isolation of those who have been impacted by a loss through suicide. We offer emotional support, help and information through our telephone helpline, information, peer led support group meetings around the country, online forum and virtual group meetings.

National Support Line (UK)
0300 111 5065
Monday and Tuesday 9am – 5pm
www.uksobs.org

Poetry for Mental Health

Promoting and publishing poetry for mental health

*"Be motivated to heal,
be inspired to write."*

www.poetryformentalhealth.org

INTRODUCTION

"Having had a number of mental health challenges throughout my life, compounded by trauma and a difficult childhood, I have always found books and words and poetry both therapeutic and cathartic, and a really good catalyst for coping when things become particularly difficult. And so I founded POETRY FOR MENTAL HEALTH, aimed at motivating and inspiring other people with mental health challenges to put pen to paper and transform their thoughts, feelings, emotions and experiences into words.

"No matter what your age, background and experience, culture or identity; whether an established writer and poet with many published titles to your credit, or an aspiring poet who has never written a word of poetry in your life, my philosophy at Poetry for Mental Health is to embrace, welcome and support everyone, everywhere suffering from mental health challenges, and help you cope through words and poetry. Get writing!"

ROBIN BARRATT
Founder *POETRY FOR MENTAL HEALTH*
Editor: *THE POET* magazine

NOTE: *For a small number contributors to this anthology, English is not their first language and, unlike other poetry platforms, I don't heavily edit a poet's own work (if I did, it would then not be their own work!), so please focus on a poet's messages and meanings and not necessarily on any grammatical mistakes or translated imperfections.*

CONTENTS

12.	Poetry by Rebecca Topham
13.	Interview with John F. Zurn
18.	Poetry by Ian Douglas Robertson
20.	Poetry by Kate Young
23.	Megan Diedericks' story
28.	Poetry by Laurinda Lind
32.	Sheri Thomas's story
36.	Poetry by Mark Andrew Heathcote
38.	Poetry by Katherine Brownlie
42.	Poetry by Linda M. Crate
47.	Kathleen Boyle's story
52.	Poetry by Anthony Ward
54.	Poetry by S. D. Kilmer
56.	Poetry by Steve Ferrett
62.	Kathy Sherban's story
68.	Prose by Hanyong Jeong
70.	Poetry by Carolyn Dumas-Simons
71.	Poetry by Tali Cohen Shabtai
74.	Poetry by Simon Drake
77.	Nidhi Agrawal's Story
81.	Poetry by Arianna Randall
84.	Poetry by Tayane de Oliveira
86.	Eva Marie Cagley's story
89.	Prose by Tricia Lloyd Waller
92.	Poetry by Gary D. Grossman, Ph.D
94.	Poetry by Prathyush Devadas
97.	Poetry by Stephen Kingsnorth
99.	Poetry by Wilhelm Höjer
103.	Poetry by Martin Willitts Jr.
108.	Poetry by Michael Estabrook
112.	Poetry by Georgia May
116.	Poetry by Nicola Vallance-Ross
118.	Poetry by Mark O. Decker
121.	Interview with Dustin Pickering
126.	Prose by Sheila A. Donovan
129.	Poetry by Sheryl L. Fuller
130.	Poetry by Suzanne S. Eaton
136.	Poetry by Gary Shulman, MS. Ed.
138.	Poetry by Douglas Colston
141.	Poetry by John Gallas
142.	Poetry by Karla Linn Merrifield
144.	Poetry by Sanda Ristić-Stojanović

146.	Poetry by Bobby Z
147.	Nolo Segundo's story
155.	Poetry By Binod Dawadi
157.	Poetry by Donna McCabe
161.	Poetry by Frances Gaudiano
163.	Poetry by Mia Amore Del Bando
165.	Poetry by Jane H. Fitzgerald
167.	Poetry by George Colkitto
169.	Poetry by Duane Anderson
171.	Timothy Paul Brown's story
181.	Poetry by Pam Ski
184.	Poetry by Jacquelyn Alexander
187.	Poetry by A.H. Waterfall
188.	Poetry by Joseph A. Farina
190.	Poetry by Mónika Tóth
191.	Nila K. Bartley's story
194.	Poetry by Sazma Samir
200.	Poetry by Joan McNerney
203.	Poetry by Biswajit Mishra
205.	Poetry by Francis Muzofa
208.	Norman Morrissey's story
213.	Prose by J. Robert Schott
214.	Poetry by Iona Winter (Waitaha)
216.	Poetry by Lesley Warren
222.	Poetry by John Tunaley
224.	Poetry by Til Kumari Sharma
226.	Poetry by Antoni Ooto
227.	Poetry by Judy DeCroce
228.	Poetry by Hasanul Hoq
231.	Lizzie Jones's Story
234.	Prose by William Penfield (Will Pratt)
236.	Poetry by Gargi Saha
238.	Interview with Alshaad Kara
244.	Poetry by Bhuwan Thapaliya
246.	Poetry by Qurat ul Ain
247.	Poetry by Andrija Radulović
248.	Poetry by Caila Espiritu
249.	Poetry by Cass Erickson
251.	Poetry by Chris Butler
257.	Poetry by Bernie Martin
258.	Poetry by Syed Ahrar Ali
261.	Poetry by Edvin Sarrimo
262.	Poetry by Dr. Koyal Biswas
264.	Poetry by Mariana Mcdonald
266.	Poetry by Christopher Martin

270. Poetry by Finola Scott
271. Poetry by F. E. Scanlon

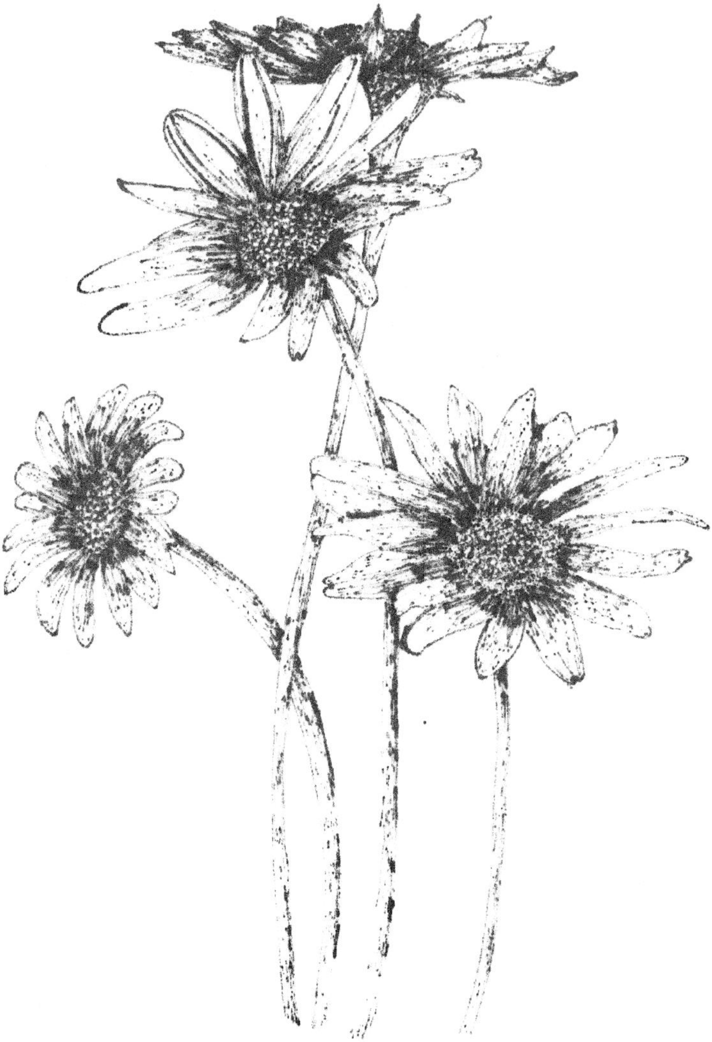

SUICIDE
Volume 2

A collection of poetry, short prose, interviews and personal stories from around the world on the themes of suicide and self-harm.

Poetry by Rebecca Topham

PRETEND

Pretend that you didn't have a twin sister
Who lived in a little flat
Pretend there weren't bright flowerpots outside
Where in summertime, she sat

Pretend that she didn't have two tiny dogs
Who accompanied her everywhere
Pretend that she didn't bask in the sun
Atop that beautiful field over there

Pretend that there wasn't a little shop
Where she liked to buy sweet candles
Pretend she didn't suffer from an illness
That -even you- could not handle

Pretend that you didn't lose her forever
And that in the woods you walk
Pretend that you sit on your bench together
Laugh gregariously and talk

Pretend that you could have saved her
That you had visited her that day
Pretend that you had helped her
And that she would still be here today

ABOUT THE POEM
"This poem is about my identical twin sister's suicide. She was my life. I hope my poem illustrates her beautiful, quiet personality. She suffered from depression, and I have bipolar disorder too, so we were able to give strength to each other. I really want people to see the person behind suicide. The act of suicide - I have found - seems to obscure the person. And so I write often in Debs' memory."

ABOUT REBECCA
Rebecca is a 43 year-old Staff Nurse based in England. She lost Debs in 2021.

Interview with John F. Zurn

John's experiences with mental illness began when he was 14 years-old. Depression, manic episodes, psychotic breaks and alcohol abuse resulted in hospitalisation, homelessness and jail. Now on the road to recovery, a combination of counselling, medication and creativity has completely transformed his life.

Thank you for talking to me John. When did your first experiences with mental health begin?
My experiences with mental illness really began when I was 14 years-old, growing up in upstate New York. At that time, the legal drinking age for alcohol was 18; so 16 year-old teenagers could make fake identification and buy alcohol, and 14 year-old students could buy from them. So I drank every weekend, and all summer throughout high-school. But, alcohol notwithstanding, I was also a pretty good student, played the trumpet, and ran cross-country and track. Eventually, I was awarded a partial scholarship to St. John Fisher College in Rochester, New York. But, in the summer of my freshman year, I had a life-changing experience: while I was jogging around my uncle's resort, I became violently ill with severe cramps. By the time I arrived at the hospital the next day, I had to have an emergency appendectomy and, back in 1974, if my appendix would have burst, I surely would have died. For the first time I realized that death was both real, and inescapable, and over time became obsessed with death. Depression began to overwhelm me and I lost interest in almost everything.

And then what happened?
Eventually, when the depression finally lifted, I experienced what could be described as three consecutive "manic" episodes. During these "psychotic breaks", I deliberately raced my thoughts as fast as possible, seeking answers to my questions about death. During these episodes I was hospitalized for months at a time, and since my symptoms were manic, I was also consistently misdiagnosed as a consumer (patient) with schizophrenia. Then, two years later, I finally made a very serious suicide attempt and was a patient in intensive care for about a week. Ironically, however, that desperate act provided the vital information needed to correctly reach my diagnosis of bipolar disorder.

How did things develop from there?
I eventually got into very serious trouble. I hired a cab from Elgin

(Chicago) to Champaign - a journey of around 160 miles, costing two-hundred and fifty dollars - so I could visit my brother. Since my brother was more interested in studying than seeing me and partying, we quickly parted company, and I ran out of money. A university counselor gave me a bus ticket back to Chicago, and when I arrived at about 2 a m, I began wandering the downtown streets directing and blocking traffic because I firmly believed I was the fifth Beatle, and that one of the group members was coming to pick me up. People from a nearby bar threw bottles at me, and a man tackled me to the ground. Before long, the police came and I was taken to the psych division of Cook County Jail, called Cermak.

What was that like?
To be honest, it was a vicious, brutal place. After about four or five days, I was pushed out the front door by two officers. I had nowhere to go, had no belt or shoes, and was told to "behave myself." I wandered around the Chicago area again for a while. I was then re-incarcerated in another section of Cook County Jail. This jail was also a violent world of savagery and despair. To be honest, I didn't think I would survive it.

How did things start to change?
Acceptance, for me, has been a process over time, and I finally realized that taking medication was a safety issue. Taking medication, and going to counselling, was a very humbling experience for me as for many people, including myself, taking medicine and receiving counselling was a sign of weakness and a lack of courage. But they are not, they are a road to recovery, and now, my bipolar disorder no longer rules my relationships nor dominates my life. Instead, it has made me a more creative and compassionate person. By accepting my illness, I have become more disciplined and productive because I better understand and manage my thoughts and feelings. With the help of my wife, Donna, I now cherish a life I once considered worthless.

Generally, how do you think poetry, writing and being creative can help people with mental health challenges?
Creativity helps redirect delusional impulses, so we express ourselves in more socially acceptable ways. For example: writing stories and poems may help channel and manage this energy into something tangible before it overwhelms. A number of us with bipolar disorder have a high degree of intelligence. However, we can't handle a lot of stress, partly because of the anxiety that is often part of the diagnosis. Creativity, like writing and painting, for example, are practised with no one else around. Working alone, we can fully

engage our intelligence without any outside pressure. In fact, the only stress we usually experience is the pressure we put on ourselves. In addition, it is very difficult to find any job that has high intelligence and low stress. Creativity gives us a chance to build our self-confidence, maintain a genuine sense of purpose, and overcome boredom.

Creativity expands awareness because, in the process of writing, we can grow spiritually by developing self-discipline. After creating a poem or story, we become a different, more mature person. In other words; thoughts and actions that once led to mental illness like "wrong turns" and "crash landings" no longer influence us. We have evolved to a new expanded level of understanding.

And lastly John, how has poetry, writing and creativity helped you personally recover?
For me, creativity also provides a sense of closure, and helps resolve festering emotions and unresolved conflicts. I think about a problem, such as a terrible memory like Cook County jail, and then I write about it, and then I often experience a cathartic feeling of moving past the experience. Sometimes when I'm depressed, I can capture the actual feeling, then describe it, and then let it go.

"Creativity keeps my mind positively occupied, so it doesn't have the chance to focus on doubt, anxiety, and restlessness."

MANIC WIZARD

Today the wizard actor plays,
a role he has created.
He energizes every cell
and wanders streets elated.
Above his head he calls the clouds
with mantras filled with rain.
Thunder and his waving arms
keep time within his brain.
This wizard knows the secret signs
in every spruce and willow.
He counts the numbers 6 and 9
and dances but none follow.
Back at home the TV screen
gives messages of grace.
Music from the phonograph
affirms the wizard's faith.
But mortals clad in black and blue

begin to close the noose.
They come and talk of things to do
beyond the wizard's room.
Finally, the wizard rides
into an institution.
Believing wizards ought to hide
they make his reservation.

LEMONADE STAND

The cutesy slogan
on my counsellor's almighty wall read:
"When the world gives you lemons make lemonade."
Of course he was paid, and I doubt he had ever tasted
"real" lemonade in his entire blueberry
life

PRIDE

A delusional prophet
sits on his self-righteous ledge
surveying his garden below.
The furious wind
rushes at him,
till his pride and his balance
      let
              go.

THE JOHN LENNON SHOW

Lennon sang and danced in the sun.
He sings and dances still.
Lifting the veil with the ritual
with only the picture-the show.
The music is great if I stay up late
and turn down the volume too low.
The images pass, the sound bites are trashed,
and only the music can flow.
Projecting my image in time and in space,
I discover the future is now.
I give peace a chance
and join in the dance,

believing that love is around.
But the storms in my mind,
deceived by desire,
I shoulder the karmic wheel.
The mantra I chant is merely a chance
for my ego to turn me to steel.

MYSTICAL WORLD

A freight train whistle
fills the clear night air,
like a ghost patrolling
some mystical world.
The melancholy droning
invites contemplation,
as the click clickity wheels
keep time in the sky.
Crickets join the gathering mantra,
while deep in the mind
the buzzing seeps through.
Slowly and deeply all sounds intertwine
dissolving the world into energy.

ABOUT JOHN
Despite his lifelong struggle with bipolar disorder, John has written and published numerous poems, short stories and sci-fi fantasy novels. As an advocate for mental illness issues, he has given over four hundred presentations for the National Alliance on Mental Illness (NAMI). In his most recent work called, *Metamorphosis: From Mental Illness to Spiritual Awakening*, John describes, poetically, his journey through mental illness and its effect on his spirituality. John taught for many years at a variety of private schools and sheltered workshops. He is also an avid hiker, gardener and social service volunteer. He has an M.A. in English from Western Illinois University, USA, and has been married to his wife, Donna, for over forty years. She has been his best friend, and the strongest element of his support system.
W: www.portalstoinnerdimensions.com
FB: @writerjohnfzurn

Poetry by Ian Douglas Robertson
In memory of my father, Douglas Hartridge.

AT 7.37

At 7.37 on a February morn
a shot rings out,
Splitting the breaking dawn.
No one hears, no one cares.
A shotgun taken to a rabbit or a rat.
To scare the pigeons off the cabbage patch.
The day halts its relentless march
For a second, a resounding split second,
To register the blast
but nothing more.
The birds fall silent for a second longer,
Suspend their rustle in the trees
but that is all.
The world keeps turning on its axis,
Indifferent to the cannon roar that
Seems to soar above the misty valley
at 7.37.

No one knows the exact hour.
They are not there.
Nor do they care
to record the time and moment.
The moment when time stops,
When a dream comes to a close.
The moment that is never shared,
That cannot be shared.
The moment when a man puts an end to his life.

ABOUT THE POEM
"My father shot himself in the early hours of the 15th February 1992 with a shotgun to his head. He had just spent three weeks with us in Greece after my mother's death. He was clearly not himself, but showed no signs of deep depression. He had expressed a wish to go back and dig his vegetable garden in time for spring. On the 14th he returned to Moorfields, where he had lived with my mother. It seems clear now that he had made up his mind, even before he flew back to Ireland, that he would put an end to his life. It took me twenty-five years to write this poem. This distance enabled me to see his death in general terms, as representing so many other sad and tragic

deaths. In fact, possibly all deaths are sad and tragic, the only difference being that his was premature. I never blamed him for what he did. In fact, I admired him for his courage. I have always believed that we should have the right to end our life when we choose. The circumstances of his suicide, however, brought home to me how alone we are in life, and particularly in death. Death is not a moment that can be shared, especially when it is self-inflicted. This poem has echoes of Garcia Lorca, a poet who, after so many years, still echoes in my head."

ABOUT IAN
Ian originally comes from Ireland, but currently lives and works in Athens as a teacher, actor and translator. He had had a number of poems and short stories published in online magazines. He has also published a number of novels including: *Break, Break, Break, The Frankenstein Legacy, The Reluctant Messiah, On the Side of the Angels* and *Under the Olive Tree,* among others. He is currently working on his eleventh novel.
E: eireian@yahoo.co.uk

Poetry by Kate Young

TRYING TO UNSEE WHAT HAS BEEN SEEN

He rose to the top quickly.
Top grades,
top of the class
top 10% at the UEA
at top of the tower
the world at his feet, but

not on top of things.
Feeling the churn
in the pit of his gut
he stands at the bar
dispirited eyes
in the base
of a glass.

He teeters, unbalanced
atop a concrete block
ready to top himself.
One step
toward the edge
a gush of air
in hair
as he

ABOUT THE POEM
"When I was in my first year at college a friend tried to take his own life. None of us realised that he was even struggling until we heard that he had jumped from the top of a multi-storey car park. He didn't in fact die from his injuries, but was paralysed from the neck down. That image has stayed with me ever since as has the guilt we all felt at having missed the signs."

SHAPELESS

the week has no shape,
it hangs from her shoulders
like a sack

the hole in the day
is too deep, too cavernous,
the sides of the hour sheer

she tries to scale ice,
trainers trimmed by hunger
in the slide of time

but snakes down in duvet,
her limpened fingers
unable to make the call

ABOUT THE POEM
"This poem was written for a friend who I shared a house with when teaching. She was obviously depressed and became more and more withdrawn. This time I recognised the signs, but she struggled to ask for help; describing her mood like being wrapped in a duvet, suffocating. She did eventually receive help."

CELLOPHANE SEA

An outline of a man
walks into himself,
emerges from depths
wearing waves. Grief,

a cellophane sea,
smothers his breath
wraps him tight
with a scrunch. Tears

absorbed in tide
threaten to ripple,
fluid as salt-spray
on surface. Hope,

an empty vessel
fades with lighthouse,
flies south with gulls
slicing the sky. Tips

of fingers cling
to edges of change,
everything bleached

in aquamarine.

ABOUT THE POEM
"This poem refers to a close relative who was an alcoholic. He lost everything to drink but sought solace in the North Norfolk coast where he could breathe and think. He considered suicide on more than one occasion as he was unable to face his addiction or make changes to his life."

ABOUT KATE
Kate is a semi-retired teacher living in England. She has been passionate about poetry since childhood. Kate's poems have appeared in magazines and webzines including: *Words for the Wild, Alchemy Spoon, Dreich, Fly on the Wall* and *Poetry Scotland*. She loves Ekphrastic Poetry, and has had many poems in *The Ekphrastic Review*, Canada. Her work has also featured in the anthologies *Places of Poetry* and *Write Out Loud.* Her pamphlet *A Spark in the Darkness,* and her *Stickleback* have both been published with Hedgehog Press. Kate's poem *Fear* was placed 2nd in the Canterbury Poet of the Year Competition 2022. Her next pamphlet, *Beyond the School Gate,* is due for publication with Hedgehog Press later this year..
Twitter: @Kateyoung12poet

Megan Diedericks' story

There are certain poems, or pieces, that I think probably every writer believes will never see/never have to see the light of day. These are a few of mine, even though most of them are also compiled in a collection I would like to put out someday soon. I even struggled with the thought of sending these in, because vulnerability and honesty so raw can be my worst enemy – but why hide, when others before me have been so brave? I am allowed to be brave, too, even if it scares the living hell out of me – my pain is my own and I think, and hope to one day know that I don't have to hide it all so that I won't be seen as weak.

Writing has been my escape and passion since I was a child – I wrote my first poem when I was twelve (I have since then gotten rid of almost all of my poems from that period, because I was a dumb kid. But that first one is still in one of my notebooks, and is titled *Sorrow is not to Borrow* – it might not actually be my first, first poem, but it's the first one I remember writing and the one - I think - that set me on this writer-path.

To close off these diary-entry-like intermissions: I can't remember how old I was, or how many years it had been since my sister died, but I do remember snooping on a computer (the box of the dinosaur-age technology had been hers), and I came across a file that had a poem written in it. To this day I can't remember what it said, and I know not if it was her that wrote it, but I like to think that it was her handiwork.

SHATTER

You left me
because you couldn't face the sickness in you –
medication wasn't your way of living.
Now, I'm left with pieces I feel inclined to shatter more each day.

Glass can never be the same once shattered against a wall;
the same way I'll never be the same after I've been forced to claw at a wall.

The reflection doesn't shimmer in shards –
I seem whole.
I can wipe my tears,
hide the body
and it will keep my secret.

Can you?

Anger burns red in your disappearance
and surrender to Death.
But yet, happiness glows for you cannot gaze
upon me, longing on my knees
for the same Deity.

ABOUT THE POEM
"This is a piece I wrote regarding my sister's death when I was a child. I only truly started to grieve the death - which happened in 2013 - in around 2018/9; I was in a dark place and, to top it all off, my last year of high-school was hammering down on me up until the point I would either hit walls, or pull my knuckles across rough bricks. I'm in a much better space now, though I sometimes still feel so ashamed for what I had done."

DEATH OVER EMOTION

The arrow grinds deeper into my heart,
recklessly tearing it apart.
The blood dribbles –
I bleed for you
and because of you.

My heart is chained, and of you – I'll never be free:
they tighten and suffocate more life
every time I try to thrive.

I'll never be able to survive
this. I'm slowly decaying –
inside-rot is never not a heartbeat away from
leaving scarlet letters on my flesh.

There is nowhere left to hide,
and no one to whom I can confide;
the arrow is drilling holes into my spine
now, and the last bit of love-colored rhine
I spared, lets out a steady-shaky final breath.

It's time I claimed
the truth so wrongfully framed:
I have to choose.

Death over emotion?
Or was there never any difference to begin with?

ABOUT THE POEM
"This is a piece I wrote during the time I was grieving the loss of a friendship - the closest friendship I had ever had, in my entire life. Without too much detail, said person knew every single detail about, down to every little thought I had during the day; me and things I never dared share with anyone. I'm the one who ended the friendship, and the reasons might seem silly, but as one of my favorite lyrics by All Time Low *goes: 'There's no love for a liar' – though I know the friendship would only have festered more darkness in me had it continued, it still hurt, and the thoughts were far from pretty."*

DEATH

I'm already dying,
though you might not see it
or smell it
or hear me beg for mercy.

Death is the only constant in my life.
I see her every day and wonder
if she'll take me away to her home of
lost souls and broken bones.
But every day, she passes me by
and lets me know it's not time to say goodbye.

Her scent is always lingering in the air,
it makes me wonder: is it fair
that I have to wait and die within myself,
while she favors those who don't deserve it?

Her hand grazes their skin,
turning what once was
full of life and warmth,
dark and cold.
She tells me, "They sold their soul,"
and I feel mine tear itself apart.

"It's unfortunate," she says,
"You would be a precious gem amongst all my rocks."
But every day, she passes me by

and lets me know it's not time to say goodbye.

Mercy,
is all I ask of her
but she won't graze my skin,
she won't draw up my contract
and she won't let me say goodbye.

I'm already dying,
though you might not see it
or smell it
or hear me beg for mercy...
but she does,
and one day,
she'll succumb.

Previously published in my collection, 'the darkest of times, the darkest of thoughts', January, 2022.

ABOUT THE POEM
"This piece is about my suicidal thoughts. I often wonder if these thoughts would not be mine had my sister not died, but I seem prone to depression – so, would there have been any difference?"

;
(semi-colon)

point.
break,

constant reminder of the
promise i broke myself.
theft of something
that should never be stolen.

heart swollen,
pain glowing
and fear growing.

my hands shake
as i catch my own tears,
a glimpse at my wrist:

point.
Break.

ABOUT THE POEM
"I wrote this piece when I was certain I had broken some type of promise to myself. All around the world, people dealing with mental illness or suicidal thoughts/attempts (or if they're in solidarity/have lost someone to suicide) get a semi-colon tattooed on them. 'It represents when an author could have ended their sentence, but chose not to.' It is a thought that I, as a writer with a brain that will not let me rest, truly appreciate. I got my semi-colon tattoo in 2018 - I believe - and the very next year downhill was all I knew. This poem reflects how I would look at my tattoo, and be certain that I failed for having such thoughts and hurting myself. I was wrong, I very often am, because if I still fight (no matter how loud I cry), I haven't failed."

ABOUT MEGAN
Situated in South Africa, Megan's debut poetry collection *the darkest of times, the darkest of thoughts*, has recently been released. Her work has appeared in literary journals worldwide, and when she's not writing, she lives in worlds of fiction with background music to match – or playing with the dogs.
W: www.megandiederickspoe.wixsite.com/writer

Poetry by Laurinda Lind

HOW WE GET THROUGH IT
After a Son's Suicide

The vast body is grounded at its pulse
and in the sap of its words.
A memory threads the blood.

Out in the world, its masks and bowls,
filters and pumps, wheels and wells
everywhere turn around the silence at its hub:
whether in fields, in yards, in abbeys, in minds.

This electricity below bedrock is a river
whose news washes all.

A body thrives on plants made of soil
and stone and stars and death, and where

we are the most ruined, there
we may make ourselves right.

First appeared in *Black River Review,* Spring 2009.

ABOUT THE POEM
"'How We Get Through It' is an attempt to find a way to stay grounded despite the suicide death of my 17 year-old son."

A NOTE I FOUND
From Something I Don't Remember that Happened Fifteen Years Ago

We had just put the lower window
back in its frame next to our bed,
the summer so suffocating that we'd
never missed it, not even the night
of the tornado when our dark shingles

shot off, bats streaking down the street.
We shut ourselves in and the wood
groaned home. The edges met. But
then the next night with no wind,
a recurrent mighty thrum pounded

at the pane. What's that, you said
as you came upstairs. I don't know,
I said, there's a torpedo trapped
in there. I think you laughed. I hope
we thought we were funny. From

this note I've found, it sounds like it
never unsettled our five-year-old son
asleep across the hall. Now, of course,
I know what tried to come, this claw
that always rakes around, raw as

black mold seeping under the green
sill. It was our two hearts fighting
for air. The way they would knock in
the night, twelve years later when
we found him ruined in his room.

First appeared in *The Broadkill Review* in the March/April 2019 issue.

ABOUT THE POEM
"'A Note I Found' is based on an old poetry fragment included in a new poem after the fact of my son's suicide death."

WHAT I LEFT AT THE BLACK RIVER

It's a hot day and my last two sons
and I go down to the river for a breeze
that isn't there, but at least something is moving:
in fact, three things: the river.
The trucks on the bridge. Our bare feet.

We pick our way around the moss
streaming from pipes in thick sick strands
like sewer sludge. I like the riverwood
that the water has shaped into soft alphabets
from languages we've forgotten how to read.
The boys are more interested in finding rocks
they can barely carry, to heave into the current
and try to rile the river more than it's already riled.

Most of the people pulled from these rapids
didn't need saving, were out joyriding
on tubes and boards while someone home worried.
Not everyone who's lost is lost. The boys get bored

and we put our shoes on to climb back up.

One of them will come back another day
to test himself against the river.
The other one never will.

First appeared in *Black River Review* in Spring, 2007.

ABOUT THE POEM
"'What I Left at the Black River' recalls a day with my youngest sons before they became teenagers and the older of the two took his own life."

INTERMISSION

In my dream, we came back
from a concert and put
all our company to bed
and then, drifting toward you,
I found smoke, black
and boiling, through a round hole
you had drilled in the living-room floor
and I looked between the levels, to find
the cellar corner furious
aflame. And I forgot
to close the door, but calmly,
responsible as Stalin,
you made the guests leave,
you called the fire trucks.
I shivered outside in your jeep
wondering if I should kill myself first,
or you.

First appeared in *Ship of Fools* in Fall, 2016.

ABOUT THE POEM
"'Intermission' recounts a murder/suicide dream."

YEAR ONE

On Easter morning I fed
my seventeen-year-old son's
funeral cake to the yard crows.
We heard they were starving,

in this spring that came
and then uncame,
the same way my son and
reportedly Jesus did.

New snow smothered the green grass
and the crocuses, and iced
the backdoor steps
and ate down into cracked concrete.
The stones someone hauled here
a century and a half ago
lay flat and still under the slush.
He is gone and I can't help it.

The crows watched, or didn't,
from all our trees. The branches
went black with them,
the sky was full but waiting.
He is so brilliantly gone.
Spring is alive, over and over.
It just can't be alive enough.

First appeared in *Paterson Literary Review* in Spring, 2017.

ABOUT THE POEM
"'Year One' describes the bewildering spring that followed my teenaged son's January suicide death."

ABOUT LAURINDA
Laurinda lives in New York State's North Country. Some of her writing is at *Antiphon, Blue Earth Review, The Keats-Shelley Review, The Lake, New Welsh Review, Soliloquies, Sonic Boom, Spillway, Stand, Two Thirds North, The Wild Word*, and *WORDPEACE*. She is a Pushcart Prize and Best of the Net nominee.
E: llind@ridgeviewtel.us

Sheri Thomas's story

"Two-Pound Baby Wins Life Fight," was the front-page headline of the Feb. 21, 1962 edition of the Jefferson City, Missouri *Post-Tribune*. That baby was me, and the story celebrated my release from the hospital after spending months in an incubator struggling to survive. At 15 months old, doctors told my parents that I had an intellectual disability. My mother questioned this diagnosis, and she fought to find another answer. Several months later, I was diagnosed with cerebral palsy. I experienced a childhood filled with leg braces, painful surgeries and bullying. As I got older, my various physical disabilities progressed. I found myself looking for ways to advocate for people with disabilities. Beginning in 2001, I dedicated my time to breaking down barriers surrounding physical disabilities and promoting full accessibility on various disability commissions and committees in Maryland, USA. My journey to tackle ableism, however, would not end there. After being diagnosed with a mental health condition, I began to unpack the realities of the stigma surrounding mental illness — and discovering how much progress needs to be made.

MY EXPERIENCE WITH MENTAL ILLNESS AND SHAME

In 2014, I was hospitalized and first diagnosed with bipolar disorder. As I struggled to accept the diagnosis, I refused to follow up with psychiatric treatment or take my medication as directed, which led to a much more serious bipolar episode in 2019 that almost cost me my life. After surviving a suicide attempt, I listened to my doctors, took my medication and, more importantly, accepted my diagnosis. Today, I take my medication as directed and continue to see my psychiatrist on a regular basis.

When I was first hospitalized in 2014, however, I was too ashamed to tell anyone that I had a mental health issue. I was afraid to talk about it because I, like so many others, held deeply internalized negative attitudes about mental illness and seeking help. This stigma was something that all of my fellow patients wrestled with during their hospitalizations: They simply didn't know how to tell other people about their mental illness.

During group therapy we were told we shouldn't be afraid or ashamed to share our diagnosis with others. But that wisdom was hard to accept. Frankly, my initial reaction was, "It's one thing to tell people that I was hospitalized due to my cerebral palsy. It's a whole other thing to say I am bipolar, and I just got out of the hospital's Behavioral Health Unit (what many people incorrectly label the psych ward)." Before being hospitalized for mental health treatment, I had only heard people with mental health issues described as "crazy," so I was afraid to open up about my own diagnosis.

ENCOURAGING OTHERS TO TALK ABOUT MENTAL HEALTH

Since my time in treatment, I have noticed that we seem to have no trouble talking endlessly about our physical health when we get together with family and friends: "I just went to see a new orthopaedist" , "I just completed a new round of physical therapy." etc. Our health comes up naturally in both serious conversations and small talk. But we don't open up about our mental health in a similar, casual way. You rarely hear someone mentioning that they were just diagnosed with borderline personality disorder, or that they're running late to a therapy appointment. This needs to change; if we continue to hide the reality of our mental health, we perpetuate a cycle of stigma and shame. If you don't speak up, someone else will continue to suffer in silence.

To do my part in dismantling a culture of stigma and silence, I will confidently tell others that I have bipolar disorder or mention that I have an appointment with my psychiatrist. By normalizing my experience, I hope to play a part in removing the stigma and fear surrounding mental health. My story is evidence of how someone can live and thrive with both a physical disability and a mental health issue. Now, I'm comfortable saying, "I have cerebral palsy, I have bipolar disorder, and I'm not alone. Many of us have physical disabilities and mental health issues." I not only pay attention when people use the wrong words to describe people with physical disabilities ("crippled," for example), but I also notice when people use negative words like "crazy" to describe those of us with mental health issues. I don't hesitate to let people know that, "I have a disability. I'm not crippled." And I say, "I am not crazy. I have a mental health condition." I was fortunate to get the help I needed, and I hope anyone else struggling will do the same.

If I can encourage one person to get help in an emergency by reaching out to a family member, friend, general practitioner, psychiatrist, psychologist, or therapist, my story will have made a difference.

MENTAL HEALTH TIPS
(I Learned the Hard Way)

- No one chooses to be depressed or have a mental health condition.
- Trust those who know you. Others will often notice changes in

your mental health before you do. I've learned trust others to help me when I'm in crisis.
- Be truthful and open about your condition. Doctors can only properly treat you if they have all the facts that they're disposal.

I couldn't "just snap out of" clinical depression or a mental health crisis by ignoring it or trying to be more positive. I needed mental health treatment.

A mental health disorder is a condition just like any other. If a doctor diagnosed you with high blood pressure and advised you to take medication and get diet and lifestyle counselling to manage it, you would. You wouldn't question the diagnosis. You wouldn't be ashamed and afraid to share your condition with others.

The more we talk about mental health, the more comfortable others will be hearing and talking about it. We have no trouble talking endlessly about our physical health when we get together with family and friends, but we don't open up about our mental health. By being open about it, we help to remove the stigmas and fears surrounding mental health.

There are millions of people just like you and me. In the US alone, over 50 million Americans (nearly 1 in 5 adults) live with a mental health condition, according to the National Institute of Mental Health.

GET HELP.

If I can help one person get help in an emergency by reaching out to a family member, neighbor, friend, clergy member, their doctor, psychiatrist, therapist, or calling 911 or 988 (in the US), or by contacting your local emergency service responders, my story will have made a difference.

NOTE: MENTAL HEALTH TIPS taken from *IMBALANCED: A Memoir* by Sheri Thomas.

Sheri's First Poem written as a child to her best friend, her Dalmatian Snoopy:

LITTLE MAN

Little Man, Little Man
I see you as you are.
Why do people see you afar?

ABOUT THE POEM
"I desperately wanted people to see me for who I was, not judge me from afar because of my physical disability."

ABOUT SHERI

Sheri's new Disability Memoir, *IMBALANCED*, traces her journey from the front page in 1962 to her current role as a disability advocate fighting to remove the stigmas surrounding physical disabilities and mental health. After being incorrectly diagnosed with an intellectual disability, Sheri was finally diagnosed with cerebral palsy as a young child. She worked as a journalist and magazine editor before transitioning to a successful career in sales and marketing. Sheri was appointed to her first disability commission in Maryland in 2001, before being diagnosed with a mental health condition in 2014. Her story of recovery and advocacy was published nationwide by the National Alliance on Mental Ilness (NAMI) in 2022. Contact Sheri to receive a free digital copy of her short memoir *IMBALANCED*.

E: imbalanced.book@gmail.com

Poetry by Mark Andrew Heathcote

THE FORBIDDEN RITUAL

A widowed woman is committed to death.
Ritual says she must climb her husband's funeral pyre
find her beloved in the blue smoking, burning ghee
her husband's head rests on her lap, ah this is suttee;
this a ritual suicide by fire on a log & straw pyre
opium-induced, honouring flames lick beneath.

They're all-consuming to her life, her mixed grief.
Is this all meant to make her otherworldly,
in this undertowed vision of heaven, sparks fly,
cries howl, soon to drown, they'll crackle, die.
Ah, this is suttee; and is a ritual otherworldly,
she glows now a goddess, ah radiant in disbelief.

Her body is like clarified butter, burning ghee.
Ah, this is suttee; this is a ritual, otherworldly
her soul is like clarified butter, burning-ghee
now she too is otherworldly, ah, this is suttee;
ah, this is suttee; a forbidden ritual, otherworldly,
sorry, I-just-doesn't think so, at least not to me.

NOT WHILE YOU HAVE GOT AN OUNCE OF BREATH

The devil waits with barbed hooks, chains cast aside
He grows tired of each failed attempted suicide
He grows weary of his countless defeats
But still, he entices calls to you with endless deceits.

So don't-be-complacent he'll never forget you
He's just been a hairsbreadth away from you.
The sand in the time glass you can never again accrue.
Even now, when you sense, there is light all around you.
He's in touching distances with talons-inbound

Wake up! Don't sleepwalk, else you-might-just-drown
Wake up! He's been there don't-you-know
Wake up! He's been there don't-you-know
Since they picked up your heartbeat on that ultrasound
And he isn't playing around.

His breath is heady hot sulphur, ah, and alas-
Sadly his eyes are an unsympathetic black oily glass
That leaves you maudlin, wishing for an early death
But like a fly-in-a-web, you won't submit
Not while you have got an ounce of breath.

And a vault full of money, anyway someone tells me
What's his hurry? Doesn't he know I'm a love child?
Doesn't he know-I'm-cut-from the cloth of his fold and creed?
I was found, swaddled in a blanket in the snow, needing a feed
Next to a bottle of gin and a cut flower, no one could name.
And since I could talk, I've accepted my share of the blame.

So I'll never-be-complacent he'll never forget me.
He's been just a hairsbreadth away from me since I was a seed.

FACED WITH FEARS OF A WIDE BLANK-CANVASS

My love for you is not in remission yet.
I have put myself on a suicide watch
but meantime, without heartfelt regret
I'll pour my debt of tears alone into scotch.

Neat, without ice or water till I forget
these wounds are like a flattened forest.
This wound where my heart's blood & love & sweat-
filled landscape aspects of a painter's orbit.

Now I'm faced with fears of a wide blank-canvass
I have to choose my pallet wisely. Paint my portrait-
a new - not knowing my subjects, abstractness,
I have to join and mend these dots of heartbreak.

Put down the scotch, and find my line of view,
each colour, medium, feels alien - eschew.
But it isn't long till I have a new smile on my face
and I put my old wares back in the marketplace.

ABOUT MARK
Mark is from Manchester, England. He is adult learning difficulties support worker. He has poems published in journals, magazines, and anthologies both online and in print, and is the author of *In Perpetuity* and *Back on Earth* (Creative Talents Unleashed).
E: mrkheathcote@yahoo.co.uk

Poetry by Katherine Brownlie

NO ANSWERS

A croaked voice and watery
cracked red eyes announced she
was fed up with life
through the half open door
it was five in the morning again
enough said
she was confined
for good

I have no answers for the
pertinent questions of life
although I am specialist
for I too am human

I have certified knowledge
pertaining to planning demographics
risk factors
predicting completion
of suicide

I am experienced in detecting
mental illness
can apply psychological rating scales
treat with cognitive therapy
the panacea of emotional
troubles

but I have left all this behind
those social constructs
of people management
giving structure but
coldnesses

I prefer now to peer
Into the soul
But I confess I feel helpless
In the face of desperation
with life

I am specialist

but I feel I have no answers

my father once said to me
I hope you kill yourself
when he was unhappy
with what I had done
such sinister mouthings
can push thoughts into action
often its others who cannot cope
with the us of us
non specialists offering
an end to their own suffering
I think I live to spite such a person

but could a machine
wish our self destruction
keeping us infantile and
unquestioning in the
pursuit of endless
infernal happiness
persuading us over time
of our worthlessness

dripping with misery
we suffer in ways
the machine can only mimic
it knows the solution to
every question
but cannot know the courage it takes to
change
to be
to understand ourselves

our suffering is part of
our human richness
and we must always cherish it
for it cannot be controlled
much like love

but to find
a lovers noose
is a deep sadness
the lure of a looped knot
spurned for now

how is hope indeed found
in a disappointing meaningless world
it can only be salvaged
from the smallest of things

I am specialist
but feel I have no answers

I can only be with
someone
in the quietness
to suffer out the new
perspective from the fretful
dark kiss of agony
to feel human connectivity and
compassion is
enough to go on
breathing

I am specialist
but feel I have no answers

but rational decisions
over our own
corporeality
are apparently socially
allowed
I have my own plan
should I need it
it makes me feel I have
the option to live
to be in momentary
happiness and resolve
to be human with
unreliable feelings
of sufferance and sorrows
deep

I am specialist
but feel I have no answers

ABOUT THE POEM
"My poem is written from the aspect of being in a helping or significant other situation. It expresses feelings of inner helplessness, compassion and concerns I have of the effects of the machine and

the algorithm has on our lives. It acknowledges that we are all human and perhaps should cherish this very aspect of ourselves, no matter who we are. Our suffering is our wealth, but can only be felt as such in meaningful human connectivity"

ABOUT KATHERINE
Currently living in France, Katherine worked as a specialist psychiatric nurse in suicide and para-suicidal behaviours for a number of years back in the UK.

Poetry by Linda M. Crate

NOT A MOMENT BEFORE

sometimes anxiety whispers:
"what if they hate me?" while my
depression laughs and says,
"no one cares enough about you
to hate you."

there are some days where i can
feel the warmth of the sun,
and other days it just feels like a lie;

there are some days i need a little help
simply to get by—

just being heard, having someone
to sit with me in the dark
makes a world of difference to me;

the days where no one has time for me and
i feel like i am drowning are the hardest—

people always say if they see the signs
of depression that they would be there for
their friends,
but people don't notice anything;

they'd only know if i were gone not a moment before.

EXCEPT IN THAT MOMENT

i remember once
after a messy break-up
i thought how lovely it would be
to be looking at the creek
underneath the water,

the only thing that kept me living
in that moment was spite;

didn't want to give him the power

to end me or my magic even though i wasn't
sure about my place in the world and everything
ached as if i had been a sky emptied of every cloud,
every sunset, every sunrise, and every bird—

somehow i kept going despite this thought,
and i am grateful;

because i didn't want to die except in that moment.

DEPRESSION IS REAL

i know i shouldn't have
let it make me angry,
but my temper rose like the
angriest ocean wave when i saw
someone on twitter claim
depression wasn't real;

if depression weren't real
then my uncle would still be here
with us—

if depression weren't real
then i wouldn't have struggled with
living so many years of my childhood
and teenage years;

if depression weren't real then there
would've be advocates or doctors
or therapists to try to help people through it.
-linda m. crate

AN ESCAPE ROUTE

i didn't know just how badly
my uncle struggled until he was gone,
took his own life because his
demons were too strong to fight
off that day;

sometimes i feel guilty because his
death made me realize i didn't truly want

to die,

i simply wanted to scoop out all of this
pain and all of this rage and all this sadness—

didn't want to be so tired and irritable
sometimes,
i just wanted an escape route from the ugliest
thoughts of my mind.

THE DARKNESS OF HIS MIND

sometimes
i just want to go
back and time to write
him more letters,

i wonder if i could put
enough love in them that he
would choose to stay
rather than leave us here
missing him

twenty three years later;

i didn't know how badly
my uncle struggled because he
never said—

he just told me that i was a smart girl
and to follow my dreams in his last letter
to me,

and that he wished he could pursue
his art full-time;

i wish that he had gotten the chance
to show his art online because maybe he
would've gotten more sales—

i wish somehow i could break open his grief
enough so that he could've found a way
to survive even if it were simply out of spite,
because i have done that

sometimes;

i wish he could've seen something other
than the darkness of his mind.

GRIEF IS HARD AND HEAVY

there are moments
in my life
where i have wanted to die,

but i am glad that i never have;

i want to live, i want to live, i want to live!

truly, i do;
but sometimes the dark thoughts
i can sweep neatly away
won't be swept away into their neat piles
or blow away with the wind—

i just want to be happy again,
sometimes it is so hard to find reasons
to smile;

i struggled for so long to find myself that i hate
the days i lose myself to my grief—

but grief is hard and heavy,
and some don't want to be bothered;
i don't know what to do with all this unused
love but ache—

depression isn't easy, but i am grateful for every day
i can feel the sun and the warmth of the love from my
friends and family.

ABOUT THE POEMS
"These poems from my own personal life with depression, and how it has impacted the lives of me and those in my family."

ABOUT LINDA
Linda's works have been published in numerous magazines and anthologies both online and in print. She is the author of 11 poetry

chapbooks, the latest being: *fat & pretty* (dancing girl press, June 2022). She's also the author of the novella *Mates* (Alien Buddha Publishing, March 2022), and has published four full-length poetry collections: *Vampire Daughter* (Dark Gatekeeper Gaming, February 2020), *The Sweetest Blood* (Cyberwit, February 2020), *Mythology of My Bones* (Cyberwit, August 2020), and *you will not control me* (Cyberwit, March 2021), and four micro-poetry collections.
E: veritaserumvial@hotmail.com

Kathleen Boyle's story

I wrote poems from the age of 12 and stopped when I was 19, the year I went to teacher training college. Thirty years would pass before I felt the inspiration to write another poem.

My 50th birthday heralded a decade of turmoil. The slow decline and death of my mum, raising three children in the aftermath of divorce while teaching full-time, financial struggles and health issues which caused anaemia and daily headaches, later to be diagnosed as cancer.

At work I was happy and in control until cuts in funding affected my position and I felt victimised, so after 13 years, I walked out one morning, knowing I would never return. To my friends and family it looked like I had lost control, but looking back, that was the day I began to regain control of my life. As it happened, during a short break in New York, not long after the events of 9/11. I wrote my first poem for 30 years and remember feeling as if I had reached into the depths of a long lost me. On my return I joined an online poetry site, *Allpoetry*. There I found a community of poets and it was like finding treasure.

After my walk out, I was referred to a councillor, but knew it wouldn't help me. Life's previous challenges had taught me how to self-council.

I wrote a memory poem about my grandma, who died when I was six. Over the years I carried an image of me feeding chickens in her garden, where her dolly tub and mangle, (pre- washing-machine contraptions) stood and she would give me a big slab of fresh bread sprinkled with sugar. The poem was popular on the poetry site, so I wrote another about my granddad. Someone suggested I write a collection and that is where the healing began.

It seemed I would need 50 poems for an anthology. Every day I delved into the past, exploring my Liverpool childhood, when life was uncomplicated. I now knew the adults in my life were going through grief and their own strife, but as a child, I was unaware of that and anyway, decided my anthology would capture the happy times up until I was ten. The project restored me. My mind was focused, exploring the person I once was, and the people who created the security of my childhood. In a way, those people returned to help me through a time when I felt I had lost touch with the essence of me.

I have moved on. The cancer was discovered after I resigned my job and, post-surgery, the struggles continued. Eventually, I moved abroad to teach and earn a steady income to help support my children and grandchildren, as well as keep the family home going. I continue to write poetry and have now written four novels.

GRANDAD

Dapper, in his three piece
pin striped suit,
Grandad, who was very old,
smoked his pipe,
deep in thought,
watching the dancing flames
from his old armchair.
Then he would slowly rise,
check his silver watch
on a chain,
and with overcoat and cap,
set off to
The Blackhorse Pub,
for a pint
and a game of bowls

GRANDMA

My Grandma, round and maternal
In her floral pinafore,
Hair up in a grey bun,
Would give us sugar butties
On the doorstep
As we played in her garden,
Amongst the chickens.

The mangle and dolly tub
Stood in the yard
Resting, while we played
At making mud pies,
And grandad inside
Smoking his pipe,
Deep in thought,
Watched the fire
Dance around the brasses.

She saw me,
Muddy, in the garden,
Amongst the chickens,

And handed out great
Doorsteps of sugar butties.

AUNTIE MAG

With saintly patience, Aunty Mag,
Would teach us how to knit,
And winter nights, for staying in,
The clicking would begin.
Knit one pearl ones,
Edged cautiously,
From chunky needles,
To make,
Bright squares, we took to school
For blankets,
Never-ending scarves
Of multicoloured hues,
And strange, lopsided,
Hole-infested jumpers,
No-one ever wore.
But auntie Mag,
The knitting queen,
Would praise them,
Every one,
And, smiling, as she
Knitted on,
She knew her job was done.

THE LIBRARY

The Old Swan Library,
where the air was thick
with silence,
was my Mother's
favourite haunt.
Escaping from the chaos
of her life,
she'd leave us all behind
to go and choose
a book.
From time to time
she'd give the job
to me,

so I would scour the shelves
to find a book
she had not read,
and I could reach.
My playmates
left behind,
with hands still dusty
from the street,
I'd find an old Victorian gem,
and on my tip-toes,
hand it to the solemn
lady at the desk
who'd stamp it with a flourish.
The job complete, I'd leave
the starchiness behind
and run to join the bustling
world outside.
At home mum always looked surprised
to see I'd found her such
a brilliant book.
Then off I'd run to seek my
noisy friends,
with library silence
ringing in
my ears

ABOUT KATHLEEN

Kathleen was born in Liverpool, England, where she spent her childhood years before leaving to train as a teacher in Hull in 1972. Kathleen has worked as a teacher in Hull, Leeds, London and Carlisle, and at international schools in Colombia, Bahrain, Cairo, Armenia and Vietnam. She has written stories and poems throughout her life, and published a collection of poems about growing up in 1950s Liverpool entitled, *Sugar Butties and Mersey Memoirs*, as well as a collection of poems for children about a teddy bear called *Harry Pennington.* During her time in Bahrain she wrote *The Pearl House*, a short story which spans the cultural divides of Liverpool and Bahrain. The story, together with her poems, *Bahrain* and *Umm Al Hassam* were published in the anthologies *My Beautiful Bahrain* and *More of My Beautiful Bahrain*. Kathleen has also written a series of children's stories for Beirut publishers Dar El Fikr, two of which, *The Jewel of the Deep* and *The Magic Pearl and Dilmun*, have now been illustrated and published and has contributed to *Love, Travel, Lonely* and *Happy* in the Collections of Poetry and Prose book series. In 2015, while teaching in Cairo, Kathleen published her novella, *Catherine of*

Liverpool and completed a revision and Part 2 of the story during her years in Armenia, where she was Head of Primary at CIS Armenia. A mother of three and grandmother of two, she has given author presentations in Russia, Armenia, Vietnam and Liverpool. Her latest novels are: *The Storyteller of Cotehill Wood, The Tale of Craggy Jackson* and *Rosie Jones.*
E: kathdodd@aol.com

Poetry by Anthony Ward

MEMORIES

All out at sea,
Away from shore,
I searched for you.

Falling overboard into the depths,
You caught me,
Saved me from drowning
As I sank deeper into myself.

Bringing me back to the surface
Where I could hear the waves swash
Back and forth in reminiscence.

GETTING OVER YOURSELF

Those adolescent memories stick to my thoughts
Like unsightly flypaper when it was trendy,
Hanging in the doorway of the kitchen,
Making dinner less delectable,
Cringing in the corner of my mind
At my sense of self back when
I thought it was cool to be crazy.
Now I see how others saw me,
I see myself clearly,
Unable to face the world
Turning my back on it,
Until it takes me by surprise.

BEING A SPORT

You want me to be a sport,
While not giving me a sporting chance
When you're at you're most competitive.

You want me to be game,
While you shoot me down,
Firing insults while I'm defenceless.

You ask me to lie,

While you walk all over me
Treading me into your pitch.

SWIMMING AHEAD

Don't you know me?
I'm the guy who held back from you at a distance.

Don't you remember?
I'm the guy who got closer to you—asked you for a date.

Can you recall the date?
When we got married?

I remember it as if it were yesterday.
While you only live for today.

For you, every day's a new day.
For me it's ongoing.

I swim out to you,
Try to bring you back to shore.

But you keep getting further away-
Until I can no longer reach you.

In the end, I may have let you go-
Make myself a vessel, just to get to you.

BEACON

The tooth aches, aching
Back and forth, aching,
Gnawing into me,
Burrowing through my cheek,
Riving down my head
With a surging pain I can practically hear,
Pecking away at the living carrion.
I stab it defiantly with my tongue,
Trying to extract it from my thoughts,
That are ranting and raving through fogged ears-
I'm a lighthouse, ravished by waves crashing,
With my head spinning ...

Poetry by S. D. Kilmer

A SELFISH SUICIDE

Why did you not talk to me?
I might have helped you see.
But you took your life.
How needy you were.

Your life is ours.
we shared our lives together.
When you took your life.
How selfish you were.

LIVING DEATH

wasted all those years.
best to sleep than to succeed,
in a life that seeks to instils fear.
in a life that makes you bleed.
best to be asleep where,
the noise doesn't interfere.

sixteen hours
(sixteen hours)
      twenty hours
        (twenty hours more)
4 days
      or 6 days
whoring time.
20 years ago.
      20 years next.
      20 year more.
dying every day.
leaving so few hours for play.
leaving much of life every day.

SUICIDE WATCH

who will stay with me?
while I slit my throat.
while I cut my wrists.

who will be there?
when I ingest a handful of pills.
or fall asleep by carbon monoxide.

who will be there for me?
who will save me from myself?
or who will be there only to watch?
I won't need a witness.
just don't need you to suicide watch.

ABOUT S.D. KILMER
S.D. Kilmer resides in Central New York State, USA, and is a retired Counsellor and Family Conflict Mediator. Writing poetry since 1968, he has been published in *Stillwords.com* (2021), in an anthology edited by Steven Sutton, (AuthourHouse, 2020), in multiple anthologies edited by the late Steve Carr, (Sweetycat Press, 2020, 2021, 2022), as well as in one Wheelsong Press Anthology (2022). His poems also appeared in the issues of *Family*, and *Poetry for Ukraine* published by *The Poet Magazine*. He is currently working on a memoir, and a volume of his poetry.
E: heardwordsllc@gmail.com
W: www.SDKilmer.com

Poetry by Steve Ferrett

SPRIT SON

Close my eyes, I feel you so close, tenderly caressing my bereaved soul
Open my all to you and you heal my pain
Pain that once cut like a dagger, eases, questions that remain unanswered, degrade,
My mortal aura entwined with your ethereal spirit
You have taught me that not all that falls is lost, but will rise again, new incarnations
Your energy by my side, we stand tall .
Born blood, lived blood and died blood, now celestial ichor flows between you and I.
Enlightenment is my journey and you are my guide - Spirit Son

THE LAST EXIT OF LOST SOULS

The sharpest of blades cut the flesh
It spurts and gushes forth, the red elixir of life
Goodbye my Wife
Last exit of a lost soul
Sleeping pills and alcohol consumed with haste
Is it enough to slip away and never wake?
Goodbye my Son, I am sorry I lost my fight, the darkness finally won
Last exit of a lost soul

The rope is sturdy and strong
The noose tightens around the neck
One last leap and the column of life snaps
Goodbye my Daughter I lost my battle, and this was the only way out, of which I never had a doubt
Last exit of a lost soul

The long hose connects the pipe
In through the window make sure it's sealed tight
On starts the engine and fumes fill my vehicular tomb
Breath long, breathe deep, soon, very soon, the longest and painless sleep
Goodbye my friends, take care of my dearest don't think of me as cowardly.
I fought the silent fight for years and knew from within that it would

end in a river of tears
Last exit of a lost soul

They are not to blame; society should hold their collective heads in shame
Where is the understanding, support and guidance, treated all too readily as a stigma?
We are sick, lost and dark and not an enigma
Help us, understand that we are not alone and can find the light
Reassure us that you will stand by our side, face the darkness and fight the good fight
We are lost souls who need not take our own life
But wait until our time is naturally right
Happy, loved, content, never having to be surrounded by darkness too tired and weary to lament
Last exit of a lost soul

YOUR PASSING, MY CALLING

You have passed from this mortal world, calling me from your ethereal hearth
Your voice beckons me, guiding my aura, leading me to you
Enlightenment, the journey that begins and ends, when our souls embrace and love again
Tired, damaged, lost, the fading beacons, empathetic ambience granted to soothe
Relight the dark, cooled souls, embrace and soothe that they may shine as they once did
Guide my inner empath, reaching out to those who struggle, bestow never wavering passion, perseverance and foresight
A gift that you gave, enriching and enlightening my life, the catalyst of evolving sentient senses
Your Passing, my Calling

MOVE AWAY, LEAVE HIM ALONE, HE'S NOT RIGHT

Daddy it's time to take me to nursery
Yes Son, of course, no problems

Lies, lies, mask my fears

It is a huge problem

Just my thoughts, no words, shield his innocent young ears
Smile look happy, act like a perfect Daddy
Cold sweats, pumping heart, on my way to his school
A journey of dread, my shielded head protects me from stranger's stares
Head down, look at the floor
Avoid at all costs everyone's burning glares

Getting close, many parents now transfixed on me with their thousand-mile stares

Children's white noise, adults' idle chatters
Do what is needed then escape, the only thing that matters
Get in, drop off, and avoid any contact at all costs

"Come on Daddy, you need to help"
Panic grows, I can't remember anything, my mind grows blank

Temperature rising, chest tightening, walls closing in
A voice from behind starts to spout unwanted advice

"His shoes don't go there"
"Have you forgotten his slippers?"
"No, no that's not his peg"

I must escape let me go, let me out, my mind is crushed I'm so weak, too petrified to speak

I want to scream, but panic has engulfed me
I kiss him goodbye and say, "see you soon".
I feel helpless and lonely, a real buffoon

Sprint out of the door, grab the push chair
Run and escape, distance myself from a situation I cannot bare
Heart is beating so fast, soon it will burst
Breathless, weak, helpless, frightened and alone.

I collapse on the pavement, cover my head.
Roll in a ball, shake, sob, wail and moan.

Grab the pushchair, try to get up.
No use as I collapse back down in a heap on the floor.
Frustration and anger, a myriad of dark emotions I cannot take this anymore

Voices approaching, teenage kids walk by, then stop.

Laughing and pointing at a floored and feeble sight
I try to get up, run away using all my might

Another voice utters words that will forever haunt, filling me with feelings of flight, but sadly no fight

"Move away, leave him alone, he is not right"

I get home after an eternity.
Look at the clock, dreading the same again, how can this be

I cry and cry hysterically, dreading the thought of doing it all again, at half past three

BLACK CANINE BASTARD

So, after months of hiding, you have tracked me down and are well and truly back in my life

The hunter and the hunted meet again in a depressive mental duel. My own Black Canine Bastard, snarling and barking, ever louder, day by day

Now every waking and sleeping moment, you have become frightenly closer, a dark enormous terrifying presence, waiting for the right time to attack.

Black Canine Bastard, in the daytime you are cunning, patiently stalking me.

Forcing me to shelter in my dark curtained, four walled existence, believing I am safe. I am penned in, no way out, your grip on me, unleashing.

Your most savage attacks come at night. My room, as dark as death, filled with the most putrid odour.

Your hunger induced saliva, mixed with my terrified sweats, creates horrific nightmares that exacerbate the daily acutest pain.

Twisted reveries of body bags from lives lost at sea. Crushed heads and body parts of brave airmen washed up on wind swept beaches.

You lick your wild sharp fanged mouth as you bear down to inflict more pain on my feeble drained body, night after night after night.

Relentless attacks knowing that this entity has lost the will to fight back, fuels your hunger. The final death blow is close, this excites you.

Like all your ancient kind and wild cousins, you carefully target your prey.

The old, weak and fatigued, those losing sight of any hope are there for the easiest of attacks.

Your unquenchable appetite for absolute mental destruction of your pray. Your menu:

My soul
My relationships
My ability to love
My strength

My will to fight and speed of flight.
All these appetizers make you fat, engorged, devouring me piece by piece. Your main course awaits.

Black Canine Bastard, an expert of mind destruction. Feasting on every single morsel that makes anyone human and in the slightest way happy.

I hope you choke and die painfully before your next humanly stalk, attack and feast, on other vulnerable souls

I'VE LOST MY AURA

Life and soul of the party
We light up the room
Charismatic, charming, engaging
Life's spirit incarnate
That's me and my Aura, folks
We are untouchable, reigning supreme
Blazing along life's highway on our Pulsating Light tour

From nowhere, the snap of the straw and an apocalyptic explosion

My personal life's reactor goes into meltdown

Something has happened
I am ill and I don't know why
I look in a mirror
I see a face staring back at me
Its eyes are black and face ashen grey
Is this the man that once was me?
Or is it the thing I have become?

I've lost my Aura

Face and body, contorted and wrinkled
The strength has gone, spirit and soul have packed their bags
No confidence, focus, energy or desire
My spiritual ambience has had its brightest moments, now the light fades

It only briefly dares to look straight ahead
It despises its own image
Confidence shattered, terrified of engagement
No light anymore, gone, consumed by black nothingness

Aura, I have lost you
Where will I find you?
What did I do?
Please forgive me
I need you back Aura
Is this divorce?
The reflection fades, and with it, my life with you
Goodbye and thanks for the memories

I hear there is a good gig going on without us, and it's playing our despairing tunes

ABOUT STEPHEN
Stephen is based in Scotland. Since an early age, Stephen has always had a passion for writing and poetry, and has recently published his first children's book, with a sequel on its way.
E: stephen.ferrett@mottmac.com

Kathy Sherban's story

From a very young age I have always felt different. As a child I never fit in with other kids. As a young adult I was a very old soul having carried more burdens than people who were twice my age. Rather than blend in, I was swallowed by the sea of people in my sphere, unable to find common ground or relate on the most basic level. I walked through life as a translucent ghost, cloaked in shame, fearful of being exposed. I wore my pain like a chameleon, slipping in and out of character as a means to survive.

    For many years the trauma of my childhood lay silent like a dormant volcano waiting to erupt. Over time, I could no longer control my emotions, my anger began to spew like molten lava with little to no warning. These outbursts seared everyone in my path without prejudice. The combustible pressure of this seismic activity resulted in many poor choices, some with very bad endings. My behaviour became increasingly volatile and self-destructive. I started smoking cigarettes at nine years old, excessive drinking and experimenting with drugs followed shortly thereafter. Threaded into the fibre of my emotional pain was an extremely addictive personality, forcing me to hide my vices in plain sight. Intentional self-isolation provided me the opportunity to turn off the noise from the outside world, living in a bubble meant to deflect more hurt. Eventually life became a quagmire trapping me in my defeated state. My world became miniscule and colourless, there was no longer a reason to continue. On December 11th, 2019 I attempted to end my life. Overwhelmed with grief, riddled in pain and mentally exhausted I breached my threshold. I called my only child to say goodbye bye then proceeded to ingest a significant amount of prescription medication. Fortunately, my son immediately recognized that I was in crisis mode so he called my husband on his cell phone to let him know what was transpiring. My husband found me curled up in a ball on the bed of our guest room. My final memory of that evening is the arrival of two police officers and an ambulance. I awoke three days later, intubated on life support, confused, angry, terrified and ashamed that my attempt to leave this world behind had failed miserably. Devastated, I realized that my demons were unveiled for all to see, exposing my pain, adding additional layers of shame to my existing trauma.

    My inner circle were blind sided by my attempted suicide, although they really shouldn't have been. I had been on a downward spiral for five years prior to my attempt, cocooned in my bedroom for days, weeks, months on end, avoiding texts and calls from friends, alienating family, living a lone existence.

Upon discharge from the hospital my hands shook uncontrollably for what seemed like weeks, I couldn't speak without coughing due to the multiple intubation attempts, both constant reminders of my failure. I realized at that time that I no longer had control of my life and needed to begin unravelling the secrets of my past. I reached out to my family Doctor to start anti-depressant medication, began seeing a Psychiatrist and a Therapist to help me navigate the murky world I was living in.

Today, I am dealing with my depression and PTSD in a healthy, proactive and transparent manner. While it is a constant work in progress,I have slowly emerged from the darkness that had consumed me and re-entered the land of the living. I no longer carry the shame of my trauma's. I am learning to live in the present and let go of the past. I now realize that the legacy of pain is not mine to carry and that the weight of that cross must be borne by the inflictor(s). I channel my emotions into poetry, releasing each one individually as it presents itself allowing it to be fully appreciated and exorcised. I use my voice to remove the stigma of mental health, speaking my truth one poem at a time, owning my narrative to empower my healing . I share my story so others know they aren't alone in their experience, I have walked in their footsteps.

Everyday, I make a conscious decision to continue my journey to self-acceptance and healing. With the benefit of hindsight, continued counseling and a strong support system I use a much kinder, gentler approach, allowing and forgiving my own short-comings while cheering my success. I remain a work in progress ….

I have included several poems I wrote in the months preceding my hospitalization. During that time I was desperately trying to make sense of my trauma, while processing my pain and trying to find hope where none had previously existed.

MY STORY

Early childhood
Confusion reigns
Family breakdown
Immense pain
Tween time enters
trauma and fear
Calamity hits
Nothing is clear
Teenage angst
Predators appear
Who to trust

No one's sincere
Arrival of Adulthood
Violators prevail
Power & money
Tip the scale
Maturity surfaces
Emotion's plot
Memories rage
Ready or not
Mid-life emerges
Crisis arrived
Mental collapse
Barely survived
Twilight years
Lay ahead
Silent ghosts
Will be put to bed

THE GHOST

Silently watching
Feeling alone
In a sea of people
Sometimes at home
Can't translate
Too many secrets
Multiple layers
Hard to interpret
A solo journey
Life in a bubble
Damaged goods
A handful of trouble
A broken child
Forever mourned
A tainted woman
Woefully scorned
Trapped in a past
No place to roam
A captive mind
In a hostile zone
Shrouded in pain
Covering traces
Nobody knows
I have two faces

Coasting thru life
Unlike most
Living my life
A translucent ghost

SILENT FAREWELL

Sweeping sadness
Melancholy grows
Change so subtle
Nobody knows
Mental turmoil
Brews within
Emotional storm
About to begin
Sensory overload
Feelings collide
Mood shifts
A visceral divide
Body trembles
Danger appears
Silent screams
Nobody hears
Life or death
A tragic event
Decision made
Energy spent

THE PLEA

Silence is deafening
Louder than words
A voice needs volume
In order to be heard
An ear to listen
A heart to believe
The senders message
Someone to receive
Eyes & ears
Spidey senses to
Transmission is coming
Sincere & true
A plea for help

Heard by few
A call to ground zero
Could that be you

LETTING GO

Destiny peace
Stay the course
Tranquillity awaits
Feel the force
Process the fear
Fight the pain
Nothing to lose
So much to gain
Shift the narrative
Gently at first
Negative energy
Will be reversed
Serenity's a gift
Embraced at last
Long deep breaths
Farewell to the past

THE PRAYER

I quietly whisper
Deep in the night
Praying to God
Show me the light
Give me strength
I beg from my bed
Show me grace
I'm hanging by a thread
Take my hand
Hold me tight
Lift me up
Help me fight
Grant me peace
Quiet the storm
Stop the chaos
Show me reform
Your divine presence
I give control

Love me forever
Protect my soul

ABOUT KATHY
Kathy is a poet and author of *Accidental Poetess, Poetic PicaZZo's, Brain Babel: A Poet's NoiZe* and *That's Amore*. Her work has also been published in several international anthologies and literary magazines. As a recent retiree, her time is spent volunteering, writing poetry and exploring the world.
W: www.kathysherban.ca
FB: @Kat's Poetry Korner
FB: @kats_kradle
Instagram: @kat_s_kradle
Twitter: @kathysherban

Prose by Hanyong Jeong

A BLACK SHADOW

As the darkness creeps in, it engulfs my mind, and a black shadow is cast from my past. I feel lost and unsure of my footing, as the footprints that once guided me are now obscured. Regret and longing weigh heavily on my shoulders, manifesting as a constant sigh. The sounds of children's laughter and birds chirping echo in my mind, creating a symphony of words.

Despite my efforts to erase myself and fade away, the uncertainty lingers, refusing to dissipate. "Thought makes existence," they say, but all I see is the glimmering light slipping away, leaving behind a black shadow. Like a hardened fossil, time seems to flow too slowly, everything that fades becomes either a light or a debt. While I know that I too will eventually fade, it is not yet time.

As a bird chirps from the branches above, it asks me about the distance I have traveled. I reply that the end is in sight, but the future appears empty, and my journey feels like a constant fight. I am trapped in a cycle of never-ending endings and beginnings, a plight that feels inescapable. Will I ever break free from this shadow's grasp, or will I be forever trapped, my story untold?

LIGHT BEHIND

As the full moon rose, marking the end of the Lunar New Year, a family of four was discovered deceased in their Incheon apartment. The father, an unemployed man in his forties, the mother employed at a restaurant, and their two young children. No signs of forced entry were found, and on the desk were three sleeping pills and a note.

"Dear Mother, in my distant hometown, I plead for your forgiveness. You always advised me to take care of my health and raise my children well, but now I must depart. I regret not being able to visit you more often. Please take care of yourself, eat well, and remember your blood pressure medication."

"To my in-laws, I struggled to survive, but my debts to loan sharks led to conflict. Though I vowed to protect my loved ones, I broke that promise, and now I must leave. My wife agrees with my decision, though it matters little. Recently, thugs invaded our home, causing my children great distress. I cannot bear to see them suffer any longer, and so we must depart."

"To the world, I thought I had reached rock bottom, but it appears there was a deeper abyss yet to be uncovered. Please do not despise us for our decision. My apologies to my children, but I cannot ensure their safety alone. If you cannot comprehend our choice, at least attempt to empathize. Tomorrow is uncertain, but perhaps a brighter afterlife awaits us."

"Lastly, to my kind grandmother who owned the apartment, I express my deepest gratitude for all you have done. I vow to repay my debts in my next life."

ABOUT THE PROSE
"'Light Behind' and 'A Black Shadow', the former dealing with the suicide of a family, the latter with the suicide of an individual. Suicide is an act of the person's choice, but it is also, perhaps, a 'social murder.' Often, the cause of the death cannot be said to be the individual's decision. It is from this perspective that I hope these pieces will allow us to look more deeply into grief."

ABOUT HANYONG
Hanyong is a South Korean, is a poet, publisher, and visual artist. He has seven books of poetry: including *Ghosts* (2011), *The Birth of Lies* (2015), and *A Thousand Years of Rain* (2021), and two poetry selections in English: *How to Make a Mink Coat* (2015) and *Children of Fire* (2021). He has published poetry in the USA, UK, Australia, Japan, Bosnia, Macedonia, Syria, Canada, Ireland and Spain.
E: jeong.hanyong@gmail.com
FB: @jeonghanyong

Poetry by Carolyn Dumas-Simons

AS A DAUGHTER SHOULD

If you were here now, I would know how to save you.
I have been vigilant, as a daughter should, noticing the signs.
Preparing for what could have been, but never was.

I missed your cry for help, I tell myself; but I heard it, I felt it, I was immobilized by it.
Your disappearance demanded a maturity I didn't possess.
I demanded a maturity from you, that you didn't possess.

Even if you had been found in time, you would be forever lost!
Still, I would try and save you … as a daughter should.

ABOUT THE POEM
"My father died by suicide on June 9, 1978. His body wasn't found until six days later. I have never really collected up all the pieces of myself from those six days he was missing. I worked with the police, calling and visiting family, friends, neighbors, driving to areas we speculated he may be. Day after day. I watched my family fall apartas we all tried to cope with extreme fear and emotional confusion. It wasn't until years later that my heart awakened, and I felt compassion for my father. He lost his power to his addictions and unsupported mental illness. Please reach out - speak, write, create your truth, it heals."

ABOUT CAROLYN
Carolyn is a retired Health Care Practitioner in Ajax, Canada. She has a clinical diagnosis of Generalized Anxiety Disorder and P.T.S.D. She is so much more than these diagnoses! Carolyn found the uncertainty of the Covid pandemic damaged the balance between her mental wellness and mental illness, and sought treatment. Taking risks at creative writing about mental health challenges is part of her recovery for well-being.

Poetry by Tali Cohen Shabtai

LIFE TAKERS

Spare death
from investing
in those who commit suicide
for him

There are no plots for products
Of the "dysphoric effect" and amount of sadness
which is also
as a pathologist for the refuge.

But still!
There are departments for the abovementioned products from A to D
and others with only a nickname "for those who did not keep up with this pace of life"*

Every forty seconds a person dies in the world
Due to suicide
Have pity on the allotment in his name
of death

"And there shall be a pavilion for a shadow in the day-time from the heat,
and for a refuge and for a covert from storm and from rain."**
And say Amen to those who committed suicide
and don't feel anything anymore
and to those who are on their way there

*Borrowed from the Shlomo Artzi song *"I was created for you"*
**Isaiah 4:10

***

I'm checking the option
Of dying on Tuesday
Will the Lord host me?

I am aware that
A person assembles venom with the aim of producing some material in
Order to allow the people waiting

In the semantic field
of all types of decrees to be completed
In a minute

That is how it's simplified –

Is this losing humanity?
There will not be enough space in such a short time to contain so many faces as the shadow of death

In fact, those who are lucid enough to think beyond tomorrow
Are finished within a range of 60 seconds
In death

Thirty times and 1 they counted me
In cyclicity /

When 2 is added to thirty
Some maintain that the "counting of wisdom" is in the Kabbalah:

They missed the complete
Torah.

Thirty and 2 are not
properly counted, it is missed,
In their abandonment

9mm calibre length 174 mm standard cartridge
(three safety mechanisms)
Glock 19

Tuesday, caught,

Hand gun.

ABOUT TALI
Tali, born in Jerusalem, Israel, is a highly-esteemed international poet with works translated into many languages. She has authored four bilingual volumes of poetry: *Purple Diluted in a Black's Thick* (2007), *Protest* (2012), *Nine Years From You* (2018), and *A Woman Like Me*. Tali began writing poetry at the age of six. She lived for many years in Oslo, Norway, and the U.S.A. and her poems express both the spiritual and physical freedom paradox of exile. Her cosmopolitan vision is obvious in her writings. Tali is known in her country as a prominent poet with a unique narrative. As one

commentator wrote: *"She doesn't give herself easily, but is subject to her own rules."*
E: chaos.t7772@gmail.com

Poetry by Simon Drake

BULLIED

I am constantly bullied, it's never ending
Every minute of every hour of everyday
I cannot go on like this, I'm contemplating suicide
I feel like there's no other way

My anxiety is a ticking timebomb
I can't cope, I'm about to explode
I have got no one and nowhere to turn to
I can't take it, I need to unload

I am the butt of the "IT crowds" jokes
They laugh as I breakdown and cry
Their comments, stab me like bee stings
It is relentless, I'm broken inside

WhatsApp, I avoid like the plague
On Facebook I am ridiculed too
On Instagram I'm constantly hounded
I'm lost, I don't know what to do

I can't face much more of this torture
I don't have a future, everything's bleak
My parents know something is wrong
I've lost my voice but I'm desperate to speak

I cannot go on, I have had enough of this
I don't know how much longer I can last
I need help, can anybody hear me
I need help but I'm too scared to ask.

TEENAGER

I am just so bloody uncomfortable
I never ever feel like I fit in
I have no friends, no one to talk to
I am so unhappy inside my own skin
I do not want to talk, I'm not friendly
How can I be, I don't have real friends
I'm not into what people my age are into

So that's where any conversation ends

Indoors things are so much easier
Outside I'm met with feelings of impending doom
At home I do not have to interact with anyone
I can just hide away in my room
Social media isn't that social
Even there I feel so alone
Although it brings me no joy at all
I am constantly glued to my phone

It is so hard and I'm only a teenager
Is this what life is meant to be all about
If it is I know I can't take anymore
I need to find a permanent way out
Then I read about teenager's suicide rates
The statistics and why they are so high
The impact it has on those left behind
Are left broken with no idea why

Maybe if I could just talk to someone
If someone out there was able to relate
I'd have a better understanding of what's going on
And why I am struggling to communicate.

SELF-HARM

Another cut
Where you cannot see
When I am angry
I lash out privately
The sting, the pain
Doesn't last that long
The lacerations and bruising
In a week they're gone
I get so frustrated
It's bad for my health
It's the only way I cope
When I'm harming myself

If I could just talk
To explain this is real
I would just get shut down
You don't understand how I feel

This all started at home
Although it sounds absurd
I remained silence
I couldn't utter a word

All of my trauma
Is buried within
The way I release it
Is through cutting my skin
I cannot talk about it
I don't have the words
If I did talk about it
Would I even be heard
I want my anger to end
I would love to feel calm
Being at peace within my body
Then I wouldn't self-harm

All the above poems from Simon's forthcoming book *Triggers*, 2023.

ABOUT THE POEMS
"I am a Counsellor and have been impacted greatly throughout my training over the last six years; writing poetry to help me process, and it has been a great form of self-therapy."

ABOUT SIMON
Simon is a Counsellor living and working in the UK. He has had his own personal struggles over the last few years, revolving around loss and grief. Counselling brought him back from the brink, and he now wants to pay it forward. He has, by chance through training, found a love and ability to be able to write poetry, and it has been a wonderful release and form of self-therapy for him. And if, by reading his work, some solace and understanding can be felt by the reader, he feels he has succeeded. He loves working with people of all ages, giving help and support where needed. For Simon, it s an absolute privilege and an honour to do what he does. Simon's first collection of 120 poems *Triggers*, will be published shortly.
E: 19.simondrake.74@gmail.com

Nidhi Agrawal's Story

Nidhi, who grew up in India, focuses on issues of emotional and physical trauma in her poetry. She strongly believes that poetry is a combination of joy and pain and wonder; a tool that keeps her going in life and is driven by the intense physical and emotional trauma she has encountered through her medical condition.

☐I believe that all forms of physical pain, whether articulated or unspoken, have serious psychological and emotional consequences that we often overlook and choose to suffer in silence.

About two decades ago, my first episode of acute pancreatitis occurred. The searing pain didn't subside and I was admitted to the Intensive Care Unit for approximately 2-3 weeks. My family had sought the advice of various doctors and had X-rays, ultrasounds, and MRIs performed, which revealed severe pancreatitis and a cyst in the tail of my pancreas. Being a seven-year-old child, I could not fathom what was happening to me and around me. The first episode of acute pancreatitis felt like a knife slicing through my upper abdomen, with searing pain radiating to my back, greenish vomit, a quick pulse, a high fever, and nausea. I vividly recall the frightening Intensive Care Units, the elderly patients, the nurses pushing me to take injections, the needles stabbing my nerves, and so on! The pain persisted and I was operated on, which is called Distal Pancreatectomy [1] and Cholecystectomy [2] in medical jargon. Unfortunately, I experienced several episodes of acute pancreatitis after the surgery was performed due to which I developed diabetes and atrophy of the pancreas.

The acute suffering has reduced over time, but the chronic pain persists, requiring a tremendous inner struggle to endure, exist, and bear the weight of emotional and physical suffering.

In his book *The Body Keeps the Score: Brain, Mind, and Body in the Healing of Trauma* (2014), American psychiatrist Bessel A. van der Kolk writes: "Traumatized people chronically feel unsafe inside their bodies: The past is alive in the form of gnawing interior discomfort. Their bodies are constantly bombarded by visceral warning signs and, in an attempt to control these processes, they often become experts at ignoring their gut feelings and in numbing awareness of what is played out inside. They learn to hide from their selves."

My biggest challenge was to confront my emotions and be more aware of myself. Of course, self-awareness is an unending process, but, once you embark on the journey towards self-improvement and finding yourself, life becomes beautiful and you acquire the art of living in the present. It involves creating a perpetual balance between introspection & self-awareness.

Spirituality & Faith: A Path Towards Healing

My propensity for spirituality is greatly influenced by my upbringing. I spent a lot of my childhood seeing my grandparents read from the Holy Scriptures and talking about the relationship between the mind, body, and spirit. The constant exposure to prayers cultivated a belief that healing and a sense of well-being can be facilitated by the constructive beliefs, compassion, and strength found in spirituality, meditation, and prayer. While enhancing your spiritual well-being won't always make you healthier, it can help you feel better and deal with illness.

  I have discovered that this practice helps uncover a true face, representing the wisdom that stimulates profound transformation and liberation. It reveals your fears, pain, and suffering, showing you that when you finally let these emotions arise and be, you begin to heal, overcome your fears, and attain love and happiness.

PARALLEL UNIVERSE THROUGH THE KEYHOLE

I was seven years old when I peeked through a keyhole
And saw the timid rug unearthing the flattened drops of blood
And tears of my mother.
Her down and out body wrapped in a ruddy red silk saree
Perished with abuse and unrequited love
Collapsing on the timid rug,
Unearthing the flattened drops of blood and tears.

The next day, I saw her in the kitchen and dining area,
Her hands stirring the omelette batter,
And her eloquent yet dreary eyes
Distracted by the sound of her glass bangles, green and blue.
She seemed to know her 'duty',
Just how to follow the routine,
Just how to unfold the language of a life that she lived in a
Parallel universe.

That night, I waited for twilight and peeked through the keyhole again.
I saw her spirit breathing behind the bony enclosing wall of the chest,
Rip-roaring the threads of the timid rug.

Her bangles bugged out of their shape to respire freedom
Dissolved into the free-flowing winds, absorbing life.

Years have faded, today, in the parallel universe,
Her body is an electric naked wire
Saturated with beauty, strength and passion,
Writing her destiny with millions of constellations
In the clear skies.

EVERYTHING IS BEGGING YOU

The house is cold tiled without your feathery footsteps,
I want to see you again,
Encompass your perfume, the spiced Japanese scent you use,
Become the breeze to your fluttering eyes,
The intoxication of your touch is the crossroad where
My body dissolves in sunlight.

Cyprus tree print on the curtains shrivels up in agony,
I want to touch you again,
Absorb the pearls that your skin scatters,
The four walls are just the walls,
They stand mute, don't paint your chuckle anymore,
The night before you left, the sky was kind,
Tonight, it screams in fury, "Sun doesn't exist".
I stand here, in a cold tiled house,
Empty-headed. Hollow. Artificial.

I want to be your lover again,
Everything is begging you, come home.

PLEASE ACCEPT ME WITH MY INSECURITY

I sketch a vermilion border on my lips with the ruby lipstick,
"You look sensual"!
"Oh Darn! What a sharp jawline"!
"Oh my God! Your lips swallow the charm of Red Petunia!"
As you read this, my heart aches to know what you think about me.
I love to receive the admiring remarks, but I am not pompous.
My senses are allowed considerable latitude to reject the compliments.
Label me precarious, I will understand why.

Someone recently asked me what my happy place is.
The question provoked me to mull over my 'idea' of happiness.
I cleave to others' approval
Like Orchids cling to the roots soaking up happiness.
I think my happy place travels through the fossilized caves of
Agony and warm fuzzes,
War and peace,
Murk and dawn,
Acceptance and denial,
Chaos and calm
To find its way to my heart.

My mind runs to find out what will make others happy.
My senses try to convince them that I am enough for them.
But, the conscience rejects the constant need to participate in this race,
The Saint says to attain a peaceful center,
It neither craves others' approval nor rejects others' presence.
But, I still expect the Saint's approval,
He says, "The attempt to convince someone of anything is a mark of insecurity".
I beg, "Please accept me with my insecurity"!

WHAT HAVE YOU DONE?

Free-flowing body odour stays and
Haunts your bathroom's bottom,
Calls you to hug your bare body and
Touch the silky tap spring sprinkled across
The four walls.
Appetency!

The raw finish of the velvet skin
When you embrace your bosom,
The shimmering pearls of water on
Your cupid's bow, and
How the almond butter oozes out of
Your frisky eyes,
Ruddy, cotton rose petals sleeping
On the curvature of your heart,
"I like the way how you wriggle when
Your mind doesn't agree with your heart".
Intoxication!

Blotting velvet under the
Running body odor presses the pile down,
And ruins the fabric.
The pearls grow dim, exfoliate and disappear when you shower wearing them.
The almond butter frosts in apathy,
The rose petals decay, and
The heart debilitate every time
Your mind refuses to give it the freedom to
Fly high, in the open sky.
Death!

ABOUT NIDHI
Nidhi lives in India. Her writing has been featured in: *Yugen Quest Review, Quadrant Australia, Girl Talk HQ, eShe Magazine, University of California, Riverside, Say it Forward, Chicago School of Arts, Lewis Clark State College's literary journal, St. Francisco University's journal, The Elevation Review (Kneeland Poetry Inc.), The Dillydoun Review, Xavier Review Press, California State Poetry Society, and Signal Mountain Review* - The University of Tennessee. Also *Chronogram Magazine, Letters* (Yale University), *Setu Journal, Spill Word Press, South Asian Today, Indian Periodical, Rising Phoenix Review, Life in 10 Minutes Press, Ariel Chart, Women's Web, Women for One, Lekh, Garland Magazine*, and *Muse India*. She is the author of *Confluence*.
E: anidhi201@gmail.com
FB: @nidhi.a.1806

Poetry by Arianna Randall

HEROES AND VILLAINS (MINE)

I won't take my sweater off —
It would scare you. Blood on my fingers
And my eyes. I can't unsee it. The mirror never lies.
Did I do that? Was I there? I don't feel alive.
Breath leaves first.
That's why I love the villains
Who fall, eventually, for the heroes.
For I have been my own villain. I have hunted myself.
I have never held a knife to the skin of another human being, but
I have thought of tweezers against my own.
The world is sharp; my hands are sharper still. I have craved it
Like sleep, like death. Why do we crave wholeness?
Why do we destroy ourselves to taste it?
The hero will come. She will clean the wounds, and change the dressings.
She shows me the sunset, and we watch the stars.
Tomorrow will come; with it, a new wind. Again

And again. The hero is coming.
I know her footsteps from the universe
The villain is falling for the hero. Spread the word.

ABOUT THE POEM
"This poem references dermotillamania, a BFRB (Body-Focused Repetitive Behavior) form of OCD, which manifests in compulsive skin picking. It can be incredibly damaging, leading to permanent scarring, panic attacks, and horrible self-image. OCD can feel like a darkness coming from inside yourself — it makes nowhere safe. Where can you run to escape from yourself? The answer, as I've discovered the hard way, is: nowhere. Rather, the focus should shift onto making the inside of your head a safer place to be, and cultivating a deeper understanding of your own heroic capabilities. I've always harboured a deep love for literary villains which fall in love with heroes; the attraction towards life-shattering light and painful truth. We are both heroes and villains. We are capable of falling in love with ourselves."

ABOUT ARIANNA
Based in the USA, Arianna is a trope-flipping writer who loves portraying the magic and strength of 'ordinary' human beings. She is

passionate about mental well-being and is a firm believer in bravery, sunrises, and witty banter. Besides looking for magic portals, she enjoys singing Taylor Swift while cooking, cuddling with her cats, and putting even more books on her library hold list.
E: ariannaj.randall@gmail.com

Poetry by Tayane de Oliveira

SUICIDE LETTER

Here I am and here I go
I hear the call
Enough trying to fit into society
Oh, I search in the frames for a picture of my childhood
And I see non
In the recent pictures around the beautiful frames
I see a face that could be mine but it doesn't feel like me
Not who I really am

Living is for the ones who can easily
Be distracted by the pleasures of life
Can someone tell me where I am?
Or where to go ...
I wonder if anything will ever be enough
If I will ever feel in control?

If I could have anything now
I would ask for patience
To wait for my future to happen

Oh, time ... If I could control you
I would put on fast mode or maybe just reset
Oh, life ... I'm sorry I've wasted you
I wish I had the will to live
Oh, everyone that I've ever known ...
Sorry if I left pain or pity
I just wish I never existed in the first place

I see the darkest side of the purest soul
Call it a gift or a curse
By this gesture, I fulfill my duty
This is how I show my love
Maybe I'm a different being
Or blame it on my obsession

Oh, mercy ... I know I don't deserve it
But please don't make get lost
Oh, melancholy ... why didn't you ever leave me?
Why did you take advantage of my frustrated soul?
Why did you suck out every last drop of hope that I had?

ABOUT THE POEM
"This is a very personal poem I wrote at a moment when I thought it was gonna be my last."

ABOUT TAYANE
Tayane is a 27 year-old Brazilian writer residing in Berlin. She has been writing since she was 13. She writes poetry, short histories and music. Her work is very personal and sensitive, often dark and melancholic, but at times romantic as well.
E: taycristinepso@gmail.com
Instagram: @dontlet.poetrydie

Eva Marie Cagley's story

For Eva, poetry has become an outlet and escape from her anger at the abuse she has undergone in her life, and a coping mechanism during the highs and lows of her bipolar. Through writing poetry, she has made peace with some of those demons, and no longer looks at herself as the victim, but as a survivor.

Anger. It is such a strong emotion, and an emotion we all experience sometime in our lives. Having bipolar, I often have mood swings that takes me high, and very low, and it is during these very low times that I experience the most anger. I tend to let things build up inside of me, and then they burst out of me with a vengeance. Through writing poetry however, I have found a constructive outlet for getting this anger off my chest, and a very therapeutic, way for me to let go of things.

Coming from a family of nine kids, we all had our fair share of childhood drama, but as an adult now, I just can't handle drama in my life, and it creates a lot of anxiety; sending me back to every bad thing that has happened to me in the past, including a long, abusive relationship. This inability to cope and high anxiety comes with my bipolar, and I have said and done some awful things during my bipolar swings. I can feel it coming on, and I if know it is going to be a bad day, I now try to isolate myself from everyone and write, because I don't like who I am when I become angry, and snap at the littlest things. I'm a walking time-bomb. But now poetry has become an outlet and escape from my anger at the abuse I have undergone in my life, and through writing poetry I have made peace with some of those demons. Bipolar is a disease that very few, unless they have, simply cannot understand.

☐ My bipolar has broken family ties and through it I have lost many friends, and have had to mend many hearts. And for many, forgiveness does not come easy. My bipolar isn't who I really am though, and deep down I know I am a very kind, soft-hearted person, who cares for others. All I know is that for me now, the best way to get things out is to write a poem about my emotions, and what I am thinking and feeling and, since I started writing poems, I have come a long way in the healing process. When things start to get bad, I now use poetry to look for the beauty in life, and search for good memories to hold onto, not bad ones.

Poetry helps me control my anger, and have closure from the abuse I have suffered, and through poetry, I no longer look at myself as the victim, but as a survivor.

THE WALL

I built my wall of mortar and brick
I made it myself and spread it thick
Not a crack in the surface not a block out of place
I dug my own hole, and I made my own space.

No windows to break thru and invade
I put in a door that I had special made.
A tornado couldn't get through
This wall of mortar and brick.

I spread it thick with my emotions
Not a one out of place
I dug my own hole
And I made my own mistakes.

But while keeping you out
I locked myself within
I should have built my wall thinner.
Not a crack in the surface.

No way to get out
I built the wall strong throughout.
I'll have to open the door now and let you in
To trust in fate once again.

In hopes that I too may restore
The key I lost to open my door.

COULD I HAVE THIS DANCE

I never knew how to dance, until I saw
That words could dance upon a page
And what beautiful music they played.
A bubbling brook, the crackling of a campfire
The crickets echo in the night.
And it doesn't stop there.
Who's to say what song is playing and where
I may be doing the waltz while you're twisting.
The smell of home-made bread and apple pie,
Fresh out of the oven,
What it feels like to touch something
Hot for the first time?

And how many licks are in a lollipop.
What it's like to sit by a campfire
Feeling the warmth of the fire
While watching the flames
Dance higher and higher.
Dancing my way through poetry.
Round and round the mulberry tree.
Duck-duck gray duck.
Ashes to ashes we all fall down.
Here we go now on a merry-go-round.
Touching the inner child in me.
Dancing-dancing to set her free.
I never knew I could go places
I'd never been or climb the tallest tree
That I could see through you
And you through me,
Or that poetry was therapy
Now I dance for humanity,
For dignity and my reality
To the blues when I'm lonely
To set my soul free,
The dance has begun for me!
Could I Have This Dance?

ABOUT EVA
Eva was born and raised in Iowa, USA,where she spent most of her time working with teenagers in a group home and at a Juvenile Detention Center as a counsellor. Working with teenagers gave her great joy, having had none of her own. She comes from a large family of nine children having six brothers and two sisters. She has always had a love for poetry. A dream came true! Her first interest in poetry was when she was in Sixth grade English class and they were studying Robert Frost. It gives her great pleasure to share her poetry with others. She says her poetry reflects who she is. Her beliefs, perspectives, trials and tribulations, hopes and despair, dreams of all her lives' journey. She belongs to the International Society of Poets and The National Authors Registry.
W: www.authorevamariecagley.com
FB: @evamarie.dunlap

Prose by Tricia Lloyd Waller

FOR JON

Curled up into a tight ball of despair in the sky blue chintz covered armchair formerly to be found in my in-laws house. I am here but not here, marble cold in front of a second hand electric fire which cannot touch me. Nothing can touch me - not now - not ever!
The phone had rang at 8.00am.
I held my breath. Told myself if I did it would be OK I would not hear those words - the words which would destroy my dreams, eradicate my future and end everything.
It didn't work the words burst out of the cream plastic wall mounted phone into my husband's ear, into his head, into his mouth and now everything is muddled, muted as if someone had upset a jam jar of dirty painting water over a priceless Van Gogh masterpiece and the paint has smudged and flowed and everything is ruined.
Everything is ruined.
Upstairs in his bedroom his cradle is empty, his pram is empty and there is a plastic carrier bag on the floor containing all that we brought home from the hospital. A tiny vest, baby-grow, bonnet and hooded matinée jacket that he was wearing when we took him to casualty on Saturday because something was wrong and he was dragged out of my arms and stuck in a plastic box and I never got to hold or touch him again and now it's too late.
Last night I prayed to God to Satan to whoever and whatever might be listening. I prayed I begged I offered my soul if only he could live I would do anything, everything for ever but ...
I have turned the key in the lock of the back door and my husband is outside. I cannot do it with him in here. I lay the yellow pages open on the table and my shaking fingers dial their number. The phone rings three times
'Hello Samaritans.'
I want to speak. I want to shout the words out to deafen the kind voiced lady on the other end of the phone but my tongue is glued to the top of my mouth and I can hardly breathe let alone speak. My heart feels like it is going to explode out of my chest. I want to speak I want her to help me but I cannot string the words together. The words should never sit side by side in a sentence – how can you say.
'My baby is dead.'
My baby is dead and I do not want to be here anymore. I need to be with him. He is just a tiny baby. He needs me. I am his mother. He cannot live without me.
But he is dead.

My baby son is dead.
Dead for ever.
I want to die. I want to die because I am his mother and he is dead so I need to be dead too.
Everything is wrong and hopeless. This house is falling down. There are gaps where the wall should meet the floor and the ceiling, where the doors should meet the wall and the bitter north wind whistles in. The roof has holes in it there is wet rot, dry rot every sort of rot. The bathroom wall tumbled down when I tried to take off the wallpaper and the outside toilet is blocked. We sleep in our coats and hats and gloves because the high ceilinged bedroom is like an icebox. The mortgage is for only 20 years because the house is Edwardian and the interest rate is sky high. We have no money in the bank and the worst thing – this house is haunted and it wants us gone and the very worst thing of all - I have broken my dad's heart and made him cry. I have never seen my dad cry before.
I want to be gone. I want it all to stop. I cannot arrange his funeral. I cannot carry his white swan- down shoebox of a coffin and watch it placed into a freshly dug grave and covered over with earth. I cannot choose words to have carved into his tiny gravestone but I am not brave. I do not want to live without him I want to die and lay with him in my arms, protect him watch him grow into a little red headed toddler/ schoolboy/ teenager/ man.
I cannot live without him. I just want them all to go away with their hushed voices, offers of food, endless cups of tea and tears.
I want him back so badly I want to turn the clock back, step into the before!
I have nothing left to live for – nothing. I cannot fall any further down into despair.
I play music so loudly that it shakes the walls. I scream and scream because it helps with the pain, I kick doors, throw things at walls, smash plates and cups.
I want to die but I don't know how. I can't stand pain or blood and I flushed the tablets the Doctor gave me down the toilet because I took two and they didn't work.
I have tried walking in front of cars but they just screech to a halt and swear at me.
I have tried to make myself jump under an express train but I don't have the courage.
I don't have the courage to cut my wrists or hang myself or to electrocute myself.
I am a hundred percent useless at everything even killing myself.
Days and nights float by and the smell of his baby head and the feel of his soft body evaporate into nothing and I find a different way of existing.

My life for what it is worth will never be the same again. I will never expect a happy ending, always glass half empty, expect the worst sort of person. Yes to other people it will look as if I am living a 'normal' life but Jon when you died so did the biggest part of me.

ABOUT TRICIA
Tricia lives in Hertfordshire, England. She used to believe in fairy tales and happy endings until the death of her firstborn son Jon Eric, who bloomed and died just like the daffodils over 34 days in March and April 1980, and her life shattered just like the Lady of Shalott's mirror.
Instagram: @lilyofaday
Twitter: @TriciaJean44

Poetry by Gary D. Grossman, Ph.D

BUDBREAK
(For JW and WW)

I.
March 22, and life pivots,
Mother Sun climbs the rungs
Of her annual ladder,
Solstice to Equinox.
In the Georgia woods,
A lone wren calls.

Ground fog rises
Through trunks etched
In grays, and corrugated
Browns. The aged
Palettes of Bruegel, Elder
And Younger

But light greens call
Spring's name. That
Boisterous child of
Each solar cycle.
Trees leafing out
Fast as snapped fingers.

Mint, moss, and shamrock.
Limbs putting on
Lime cloaks, ripening
To olive, like my
Skin, aged from
Ivory to speckled tan.

II
Leaf-fall is months away,
And that final winter.
Three score and ten, yet
Not for all. Wyatt, 21,
Who dove again, and again,
Into a chemical sea.

Arms extended, we
Reached through

Funneled currents, and
Wrestled the ten-armed
Reaper, but the
Boy surfaced no more.

III.
Kids grow up, old
Friendships crack, like
Greenstick fractures.
Reunions of convenience,
Neighborhood shops,
And the local pool.

At the memorial,
She broke when I held her,
Salty rain on my shoulder.
And a burden, like
Lot's wife. Surely I
Could have done more.

But the buds will
Break again next year,
And the next. Woods
Bursting green; late March
Or perhaps early April.

First published *Last Stanza Poetry Review #4,* 2021.

ABOUT GARY
Gary is Professor Emeritus of Animal Ecology at University of Georgia, USA. His poetry is published in over 30 reviews including: *Verse-Virtual, Your Daily Poem, MacQueen's Quinterly, Poetry Superhighway, and Delta Poetry Review*. Short fiction in *MacQueen's Quinterly* and creative non-fiction in *Tamarind Literary Magazine.* For 10 years he wrote the *Ask Dr. Trout* column for American Angler. Gary's first book of poems, *Lyrical Years* is forthcoming in 2023 from Kelsay Press, and his graphic novel *My Life in Fish: One Scientist's Journey* has just been released.
E: todaysecologicalsolutions@gmail.com
W: www.garygrossman.net
Blog: www.garydavidgrossman.medium.com

Poetry by Prathyush Devadas

HER DEMON

The thin veil of fog has gone, alas!
In the moonlight, I see you,
Naked all over,
Clothes of supposed ego and revenge,
All shed off;
In broad daylight,
I've cursed your being,
But even in today's darkness
Your purity gleams;
I miss the times I thought we were meant for each other,
Now I'm just a severed kite flying hither tither.

Your hair all over the raging wind,
Your face; so pale, like the cloud-dressed moon,
Your fingers, so lifeless,
Like drooping leaflets,
Your smile; so rare
Like a perfect diamond,
Your cries, they echo
In the corridors of my heart,
Cries of helplessness,
Cries of turmoil,
I jabbed at your heart,
With a double-edged sword;
Now I'll bleed my last,
Till my dirty skin,
will rot, all over,
And teach new grass
To grow,
And by death;
I shall fulfil
One last good deed,
And you can laugh,
At my rolled-up eyes,
As they roll off the earth,
Like two black balls
Rushing downhill,
And falling into the river
Of the tears that you shed.

Wrong; have I been
To your poor little soul,
Yet, strong, have you been,
Through your drizzle of tears,
Strong enough to kick hard,
At my rusty coffin;
Yet, you shall kiss me goodbye,
And cry all over my monstrous being,
The shower of my wrong-doings,
Now a stream from your eyes,
Which shall drown me
To a second death,
Or throw me onto a rock,
Break my head,
And let the blood flow
On the altar of your happiness
The demon shall rest for last.

THE PATH OF LIFE

The sun lingered on the cliff's deadly end,
Threatening to fall off and set on my times,
Disrupting the bells in my heart and their chimes,
Lusting for an easy way out,
Yet stumbling on a rocky route,
Filled with guilt and unsettling fear,
Yet wading unfazed while shedding a tear,
Across the river of reflections,
Across the throes of afflictions.

My soul's window was shut close,
Yet flurries of thoughts flowed like prose,
Through the fortress that they call mind,
Reins sprawling as tightly as they bind;
Reins of sweet little mental images,
Of parents and their unwavering hopes - emotional luggages;
A wave of overwhelming fear swept, unfazed,
The fear that the seeds I bore
Shall vanish into unpleasant lore;
The seeds of my actions, emotions, decisions,
Altogether affirming my human position.

As the blade tried to maim,
Sever the roots of life,

It fell down motionless,
blunt-pointed and destroyed,
By the invisible power
Of everything that I cared for,
Lived for, and then too, wished to live for;
I strode on, unwillingly, across the path of life,
Now proud and tasting a fruit so ripe,
The fruit of life that millions fight for -
Cancer patients and malnourished children across the globe,
A knife in their hearts as they crave to wake,
To more sunrises and moonlit nights,
To walk across the path of life
That I tried to abandon,
The most selfish act humanly possible.

ABOUT THE POEMS
"These poems are based on the suicidal thoughts I had when I had a major setback in my love life."

ABOUT PRATHYUSH
Prathyush is a 22 year-old medical student currently residing in Kerala, India. He completed his secondary education from Chinmaya Vidyalaya, Kannur, before joining the Medical Doctor program (MD) in Lviv, Ukraine. The Russia-Ukraine war led to disruption of his education, and he is currently looking for options for continuation. In the meanwhile, he enjoys writing prose, reading books and listening to music.
Instagram: @je.suis.prathyu

Poetry by Stephen Kingsnorth

COMMITTED?
From a sufferer of Parkinson's Disease

Most seem to say the night's a drag,
though I wrest vape from pillow, slip,
and dangle legs from slippy sheets
so they can kick through bedside air,
until I slide, led heavy head,
matt beard to board, so down to rest.

It's evenings when the hands crawl slow -
a windup, time mite, slide, minute,
of minute overtaking hour
then ambling, climbing to the top.
They creep, long watches of the light,
while timepiece, not to be disturbed.

I have my glass of tumbler thought,
pills, tablets where my writing wrought,
a would-be wordsmith stymied, caught
in time-warp, blackhole, worm event.
Who cares, like readership of three,
triple, trinitarian, me.

I write to save the counsel fees,
to push back on allotted time
when I have had enough of me.
I've known the husband taking leave,
brainstorm redressed, unbalanced mind,
but wonder if my time has come?

The plan is laid, strategy formed,
with due disguises in the fray,
to cause as little pain for loved,
avoid committed, termed a crime.
I'll make fake news, a coverup,
a cocktail, bottles down the drain.

But did I follow through that dream,
as kids and grands, in hinterland -
no grief at stake, all be it sad?
You may search columns of obits,

the graveyards, scattered ash instead -
but I'm left hanging, swinging legs.

ABOUT THE POEM
"Writing 'COMMITTED?' in my particular metred style enabled me to express my inner turmoil and logical processes as I worked out (also with the very supportive GP) what consequences would result, and I accepted the fairly heavy medications (including addictive ones) that she and the Parkinson's Consultant recommended. It does not mean that the drivers have gone away, but I reread this poem when that happens, and am reassured as I read my own self-arguments rehearsed again! And similar arguments may fit with the situation of others."

ABOUT STEPHEN
Stephen (Cambridge M.A., English & Religious Studies), retired to Wales from ministry in the Methodist Church due to Parkinson's Disease, has had pieces published by on-line poetry sites, printed journals and anthologies.
Blog: https://poetrykingsnorth.wordpress.com

Poetry by Wilhelm Höjer

HALO'S IN THE NIGHT

There walks a man on the street.
His town is the world's town.
Where others talk, he communicates
his joy and pain with silence.

But those who can hear and see,
knows all he goes around and thinks.
O rising moon! O lady moon!
Through streets he won't exchange
for all that others seem to forget.

If somebody, sometime, saw him there,
as he walks there now, my love,
then the world would receive him
as the gift they did not see.

What is it with him, my friend?
His wisdom lifts him high over land
into all that his heart can do -
it was not meant for him ...

It's more than others who seek
through books he read and threw away.
O risen moon! O Holy moon!
Wisdom is sorrow of the heart -
beautiful is the one who knows - that

no other pain is greater than love.
He teaches me what I think I know:
how light shines on after the sun goes down,
how every night will beget a new day.

An old black-cloaked woman sits and thinks
about that time when she was young ...
A little iron bench is her throne
and she knows that life exists.

For even if old age is hard,
she sees a little girl and a boy ...
Good moon! Good moon! O friendly moon!

All of us people are similar, before
the end we become ourselves.

If somebody, sometime, saw them there,
as they appear there now, my love,
then the world would receive them
as the gifts they did not see.

THE DOORWAY

How quickly the doors of perception change,
but quietly,
without thunder and lightning,
almost unnoticeably.
Yet what has changed?
When life is still life,
the sun the same sun,
the clouds the same clouds.
When possessions are not more than that,
when friends are friends,
when the joy of seeing and hearing, giving and receiving,
is the same.
Then nothing has changed,
nothing has been lost or found.

All is of a greater will.
All is a gift.
All is to be
in this world
for as long as it lasts.

So what has changed so quickly?
Everything and nothing.
We are all the same -
created to share the light,
created to die -
another day.

CANTO 33

The light in the night
from a distant shore,
the life that's in sight

is a lifetime more.

Our minutes are given.
But beyond this gift,
which gives as leaven,
and so rises to lift,

is always something more,
something so true,
something we see and implore,
something found in a clue.

To seek life and to see,
almost nothing of everything.
To live, cry, smile and be,
to know we fell from something.

But know nonetheless,
all you do, all you are,
resembles yourself. Yes,
as the sun is a star.

Perhaps only now,
you see what you know,
past the why and the how,
it is love, watch it grow!

Light enhances everything.
Darkness made life and man.
When we truly learn to sing,
we'll see how it all began.

Now hear it be said,
know it happens for sure,
when each night is fed
with life, it lives more.

Sing, my good friend,
the night does you good,
sing and then sing again,
to be better understood.

I listen when you croon,
the night sings in tune,
as if it were you,

yes, as if it were you!

ABOUT THE POEMS
Wilhelm's stepsister committed suicide in January 2020. The last text between them was an exchange about the St. Francis poem: *Canticle of the Sun*. After her suicide he refused to understand her motivations, but he was haunted by a need to not let her suicide overshadow her life. He came to an insight that if we think of the good things shared together, then death is not so far apart from life. If poetry is to retain a childlike view of the world, full of wonder, then these poems is an attempt to remember another time, but also to prevent another suicide. Hope is to trust in the promises of life against ball odds.

ABOUT WILHELM
Wilhelm in Stockholm, Sweden, into a diplomat family. He grew up between America and Europe and studied philosophy and journalism at the Pontifical Angelicum University in Rome, Italy. While employed at the Vatican City, he was an editor on the International News Desk of *Vatican News* (2008- 2015). Wilhelm has also appeared in the *Epoch Times, Dagbladet, Katolskt Magasin*, and on *The Proverbial Lawyer Radio Show*. He is currently a high-school humanities teacher at the St. Vincent de Paul Academy in Missouri, USA.
E: wilhelmhojer@gmail.com

Poetry by Martin Willitts Jr.

THE MONARCH

After my friend died, I opened a white envelope,
and a single Monarch stretched, twitched
its monogram wings, flew among other released butterflies
filling the fields with hundreds of stories about loss.

I walked into the speechless silence,
allowing the total quiet to speak to about pain.
I could not even murmur like butterflies in flight.

It took years before I could say anything
about the untimely death that can snatch any of us,
lift us away.

I recall fly-fishing with him on the banks of a small lake,
flicking our lines into the sky. Our lines arching in a tiny sound
less than a butterfly opening and closing its wings.
Our bobbins would plop up, a repressed burp from the lake.
They would float like slow dreaming clouds, until a tug,
made us reel furiously to see if the fish was a keeper.

The fishing that wasn't important, nor the size of the catch,
nor the long patches of nothingness
as quiet as leaves in a slight breeze. We sat
as close as two boys can sit without touching, letting the day
drag its carcass across the sky. It was about being in a day
that drifts, aimlessly as a butterfly. The day
dragged the quiet, and we'd ignored anything else.

Living in the moment shows how the sky
and water can match.
Sometimes clouds open envelopes of rain.
Nothing matters in the moment, except the moment.

INCENSE COVERS THE TRACE OF EVERY SIN
(Clairsentience is the ability to predict with intuition)

Something told me to stay home the day my friend leapt
high enough to die.   I complained about a tummy ache,
          like a mule kicked me.

My father said I was avoiding the train trip
              he had planned   forever,
    my pain   my imagination.

I felt something was wrong: my friend went to practice mass,
        following the priest   chanting in Latin
        trying to discern   if the faith was for him
              as he questioned faith.

The signs were there: my friend's head in contrition,
        meek words   edging in shadows:

but we were both ten and trying to fit into adult shoes:

        I have excuses, uncertainty,
            not listening to what was not said,
                his eyes glancing elsewhere.

       I ignored what I felt: his shame   my shame
           the whole circle of guilt and avoidance.
He had the secret rites of the church   I had mumbled prayers
        He had the Catholic ash mark
            for salvation   or so I thought

        (For you were made from dust, and to dust you shall return)
          "In Genesis," he recites by rote
            without emotion or emphasis
              (a clue I missed).

In retrospect, his suicide makes sense knowing his sexual abuse,
       the way he wanted to kiss other guys
           the way I backed off, horrified.
       The way the priest denied he did anything wrong.

After this death, the church whisked the priest to another parish
       continuing his legacy,
           boys counted as rosary beads.

I can forgive my friend   even my response as a child
my friend leaping to escape this world
the church unwilling to bury a suicide.

       I can forgive them all

       I once saw the priest wearing his black shirt,

                        white collar,
                        holier-than-thou
at a store, expecting him to bless the bread, have it multiply,
serve it to the poor.
          My friend clung to the priest's shadow like leprosy.

          I should have noticed then,
but my father was distracting me,
                    nattering about the train trip
          (I have suppressed where we went that day).

My mind said   Never mind.

My friend and I rode ten-speeders earlier,
          lazed in a field, naming cloud-shapes:
                    he saw the Eucharist
          I saw a gravestone with a crying angel

                    I should have known then,
                              my head tinging,
          warning like railroad crossing red light
          before the bars go down.

He wanted to tell me something   couldn't spit out.
          I should have insisted,
                    but I was naming shapes:
                              a cross
                              a pierced arrow
                              a confessional booth
                              a kneeling child

          an approaching black cloud like a priest.

GORM

I'm stacking some peculiar, shaped stones
                on top of   each other
to make a cairn,   and one of the stones
        is a smoky quartz, gorm.
Although I could use this gemstone for jewelry,
          some believe it can disperse fear,
                    lift negativity   and depression,
eliminate suicidal feelings.   I'm adding it
          to this burial marker,   this practice

of balance   and   awkwardness.
              This is my landmark for the cremation ashes
                           for a friend who jumped.
Balance in the world depends
                           on small toeholds.
         For a while, my friend tottered, edging,
looking like he might re-set,   change his mind.
              For a while longer, he was an odd flightless butterfly,
                      frantically holding air.
         It takes a while to set these awkward rocks,
                   takes precision to set them right.
The rocks wobble like he did.
              I select the gorm, because it stands out,
                      its brown transparency almost calming.
I'm making this cairn in the balance of the day
         when night begins falling
                   straight down
                             vertically.
There is something simple to stacking uneven stones —
              the quiet of them,
         the awkwardness of the stones and death.
                   Each stone, unmarked, unremarkable,
                             is stacked memory.

ABOUT THE POEMS
"These poems are about a friend that committed suicide when he was 10 years old. The poems are from a larger chapbook collection I have been working on for years called, 'Lepidopterology Prayers.' He was an altar boy molested by a priest. The priest was a collector of butterflies (Lepidopterology is the study and collecting of butterflies). I am in my 70s now, and I still think of that boy going up to the bell tower and leaping. I remember the good times we spent on bicycles. I was asked to testify, but back then no one wanted to put a priest in jail, and they did not believe a ten-year-old me. The only other thing I want to mention is that the stacking of rocks for a grave marker is a cairn and Gorm is a particular gemstone with 'psychic powers' which I included into the poem."

ABOUT MARTIN
Martin is a retired Librarian living in New York, USA. Winner of the 2014 Dylan Thomas International Poetry Contest; Rattle Ekphrastic Challenge, June 2015, Editor's Choice; Rattle Ekphrastic Challenge, Artist's Choice, November 2016, Stephen A. DiBiase Poetry Prize, 2018; Editor's Choice, Rattle Ekphrastic Challenge, December, 2020; 17th Annual Sejong Writing Competition, 2022. He has over 20

poetry chapbooks including National Chapbook Contest winning *William Blake, Not Blessed Angel but Restless Man* (Red Ochre Press, 2014) and *Turtle Island* Editor's Choice Award for his chapbook, *The Wire Fence Holding Back the World* (Flowstone Press, 2016). He also has over twenty full-collections of poetry including National Ecological Award winner for *Searching for What You Cannot See* (Hiraeth Press, 2013) and 2019 Blue Light Award winner *The Temporary World*. Forthcoming books include *Ethereal Flowers* (Still Point Press, 2023), and *Rain Followed Me Home* (Glass Lyre Press, 2023).
FB: @Martin Willitts Jr.
W: https://nyq.org/poets/poet/martin-willitts

Poetry by Michael Estabrook

MARIA

*.he felt the whole world weighing down
upon him a modern Sisyphus as the sky
turned black his hands cold as crabs ...*

Bobby! For crying out loud!
Your cousin Maria is beautiful!
I just talked with her on the phone.
She's also a brilliant psychotherapist
and personable I can tell
she's caring and thoughtful
considerate, and kind.
I found her picture on Facebook.
Dude! I'm not kidding!
She's simply beautiful!
You should see her, you've got to see her!
What have you done?
Where have you gone?
You'd be so happy to still be around
just to spend time
with your cousin Maria,
to see her, talk with her, touch her hand,
breathe the same air she breathes.
I know you would. I know it.
Bobby! For crying out loud!

BUM KNEE

*... scared me when my brother
joined the Hemlock Society
because suicide runs in families ...*

As Uncle Bill got older
his bum knee got bummer.
One evening
after finishing half a plate
of spaghetti and half
a bottle of whiskey
he sat at the edge of the bed
leaned into his shotgun

cold barrel hard
against his heart
("Not his head,
he wanted a funeral"
Uncle Bud said.)
and squeezed one off
splattering blood and bits of himself
all over his sister Kay's nice new
flower-print wallpaper.
He didn't leave a note.

SHE'S RAGING AT ME FROM THE INSIDE

*"I can't live on
this way any longer.
I am desolate."*

Back in 1932 my grandmother
turned on the gas in her stove
didn't bother lighting it
abandoning three little daughters sinking her talons
into me from across the decades
the chiseled brevity of her existence
a staccato symphony pinioning me
forbidding my flight from the resonance of her life.
And she was so beautiful, too, odd I know
for a man to say about his own grandmother
but when she ended herself
on such a grievous note
she was only 26 leaving behind
a scattering of darkening photographs
of her bright brown eyes, wavy black hair, white teeth
perfectly shaped lips and smile
tiny cleft in her chin
so soft and delicate.
And that's how she'll remain in perpetuity
for me, 26 and beautiful.
But never mind all that
what I'm trying to say here is
there's such a strain inside me
I can't begin to tell you.
She's here inside me, you see
I can feel her squirming around, hear
her screaming, shrieking in fact, like crazy

from inside me raging to get out, raging!
Jesus, but this is hard to explain.

SYLVIA

... Sylvia Plath pithy and pure I want
to hold you close, hear your plaintive voice
whispering in my ear ...

On Nauset Beach searching for Sylvia
with her high words, right and perfect
archaic and pure like her soul

She's not in the waves
fighting them as usual
rebellious, headstrong against the tide

Rather than finding her rhythm
going along with the flow
like the gulls above and the seals below

Perhaps she didn't come here today.
She remained behind
to finish her poem

But no, I see her in her sand chair
lying still, sleeping perhaps
open book of poems across her chest.

POETRY
"For the first time I understand the meaning of suicide ... God, how pointless and empty the world is!" Malcolm Lowry (1909-1957)

Bobby #1
I should've been there
to stop him
but his cousin Maria, a psychotherapist, said
nothing anybody could do
his depression swallowed him alive.

Bobby #2
What can you do about it really?
But I'm still mad at him.

We had stayed in touch our whole lives
up until the end.

Only 26
So despondent that she closed herself
in her mother's kitchen
opened the jets on the stove.
She was beautiful too and only 26. Thankfully
she left the children at her sister's.

Muriel
Clutching to life like a lizard
inside a glass tank knowing
she'd be falling off sooner
not later as she might have preferred.

Crabs
He must've felt disconnected from life that final day
the world weighing inconsolably on him
a modern Sisyphus
as the sky turned black his hands cold as crabs.

ABOUT THE POEMS
"My grandmother, an uncle, one of my best friends ... that's enough suicide for any one person I think. My brother too talked about it quite a bit, even joined The Hemlock Society. I suppose I can understand the desperation that might drive one to take such a drastic step, blinded by the pain, unable to think clearly, to consider what it does to the people left behind. That's the worst outcome of suicide – how it impacts those loved ones left behind – anger, fear, confusion, and wondering forever if there might have been anything you could have done to prevent it."

ABOUT MICHAEL
Michael lives in Massachusetts, USA, and has been publishing his poetry in the small press since the 1980s. He has published over 20 collections, a recent one being *Controlling Chaos: A Hybrid Poem* (Atmosphere Press, 2022).
E: mestabrook@comcast.net
W: www.michaelestabrook.org

Poetry by Georgia May

THE PHOENIX DROWNED IN THE OCEAN

whenever i'm sad, i think of our day on the beach, you say
walking me through some late-night breathing techniques
empty bellies, warm beer
full up on a caramelized sea bliss
my good place turned bad
because still
i'm shaking sand away from the corners of my heart
no longer blissful
but stubborn and gritty
that once warm beer turning to ice-cold wine
alone in the late-September bite
in cheap cans
unshared

the ocean is churning and quartzy
while a strange man sets newspapers on fire beside me
it's midnight but i'm not scared of him
how can i be? when just over there
not so long ago
two benches down and south-to-the-sea
i downed those cans with a couple six packs of something else
not beer
but something white for this lifelong headache
the memories that these pebbles hold
reduced to shoplifting paracetamol on a Monday night

when i google how long it will take
the answer horrifies me
why didn't i choose sleeping pills? the same as in the movies
then it gets even darker and i can't open my eyes
not because of the sand but something chemical
i hear footsteps crunch on stone
              suddenly
i'm in a car
driving, driving
fast like i used to love in those twilight summers
high in the back seat with no belt on
i guess i'd always walked along the edges of life
craved the thrill of it
but never expected i'd jump off altogether

until the night you took a match to my life

i was hoping for a phoenix but the ash turned to quicksand
and me drowning in it, beside the ocean
i hear my mothers voice
your life is precious
when did she get here?
her words mingle with the sound ambulances and—
i think someone is crying
when i do open my eyes again
i'm looking at a different pretty boy
a sparkly new one with the same bad habits
our lips are chapped from cocaine and kissing
but nothing he says can reach me
there's a crosshatch in my brain where everything falls through
truth, lies, love—how am i to tell the difference?
it all means nothing after you.

GUILTY CONSCIENCE

the doctor asks has somebody hurt you?
and i wonder if it counts if they didn't mean to
he leaves bruises on my face when i ask him to be gentler
blames it on passion and forgets two minutes later
he laughs when i push him away
such an overaction to a silly little love bite
the ones he leaves without consent every night

does it count as abuse if they punch the things around you?
break their own bones and blame it on you
who was stood in the kitchen two doors down when it happened
i tell him to sleep on the sofa
and on his way out he mutters something about boiling water
something about pouring it over me in my sleep
and then that laugh again
when i get upset
over such a silly little joke

what a cruel way to talk about the one you "love"
when i'm sitting at a bus stop alone on new year's eve
and you're telling the whole garden of a stranger's party
that i'm probably out with some boy inside me
but now i know it was just your guilty conscious talking
because you were the one inside different people

ones with flatter stomachs and younger minds
more easily bent
who can eat takeout without getting stretch marks
the ones that mingle with evidence of self-sabotage
slashed out on the skin

i have a bad night
and you tell me you know by pinching the place that's just stopped bleeding
say how pathetic it is
then kiss me there two hours later
promising to walk me to therapy next week
except you didn't
because then i caught you inside different people.

RAIN

i forget myself like a cup of tea left on the side
a comfort turned cold
because sometimes comfort can feel uncomfortable
like borrowed joy
it slips out of my hands like a bar of soap

after so long in a storm
a clear sky feels only temporary
i have my umbrella ready at all times
perhaps i even want it to rain
i'll know what i'm doing then.

SUMMERTIME

every night i tie myself a noose
and every morning take it down again
every night i drink myself into a good mood
and out the other side again
even in my dreams i am sick
with that feeling of catching up with yourself
catching up in summertime
when the pain of wearing shorts in June
is worse than the thing that drove you to it in the first place
now that my mother's making lemonade and pretending not to see evidence of weakness
of waving a white flag at the devil and letting him leave claw marks

all over you
but what's life without a few scratches on the surface?
a little feedback, a little turbulence
my friends find a photo of me from years ago
all skin and bone and empty spaces
and say this was when we were worried about you
but now i drink beer instead of starve in summertime
i don't cover myself in shame to cook through mid-July
i do all this
so that they need not be worried anymore
never again in summertime.

ABOUT THE POEMS
"Many of these confessional poems were written following the end of a toxic relationship that made me fall back into bad habits, and I used writing as a way of dealing with/getting out of it."

ABOUT GEORGIA
Georgia is a Portsmouth-based film journalist with a handful of micro-poetry publications (both in print and online). Her work - primarily scripts and experimental short films - has also been Officially Selected by over a dozen film festivals around the globe.
E: georgiabrawn@hotmail.com

Poetry by Nicola Vallance-Ross

LOST

The twigs crunch below me, as I attempt to trick my brain
into thinking differently.

The black treacle has crawled back into me marred with a slithering agitation
that's going to furnace through every connection I have,
leaving nothing but shards of potent black dust in its wake.

People wax lyrical about bravery and inspiration in my dealings with
the devilish treacle as I claw at my scalp
looking for the easy way out.
They reassure each other that I'm strong,
that I'm successful. Simply another hurdle for me.

The bridge,
the water,
five hundred and twelve feet of temptation. Feet dangling over the edge, in this Scottish winter, just hoping to quiet my brain.

Let go.

Maybe there would be happiness
if my bones were to shatter across that water. The Forth.

And you, you,
would remember the me before the neediness, blackness and agitation.
Before incessant messages and crisis calls. Before the madness.

The me that was free of acne and agitation, of mood stabilisers and mania
and of this dark, deadly depression.

Back when I smiled wildly and meant it,
when my eyes glistened.
When I could concentrate, build relationships, succeed.
When the world leaned towards me.
When I provided you with warmth, not fear.

Before bipolar.

ABOUT THE POEM

"I wrote this poem during a very dark time in my life. Often, during dark times I would write to get my feelings out which would make me realise I could get through them. I was diagnosed with bipolar disorder in 2021, following a period of depression during the pandemic. I was shocked at first, and felt somehow defective. I always suspected that there was something 'different' about me, not specifically mental health related, but I would go through periods of intense energy and motivation followed by a very deep crash into depression. This would happen when I was under strain or stress, however the depressions were short-lived so I tolerated them. I've always enjoyed writing and started writing poetry around age 12. I was inspired by Sylvia Plath as a child. I would strive throughout my early life to succeed and escape my upbringing (which was chaotic). I believed if I had a degree and a good job that somehow that would be me 'fixed'. Despite my illness, I have overcome many mental health challenges, and have managed to find happiness and success in life. Bipolar disorder is often interpreted wrongly and has such stigma attached to it. However, I strongly believe that with the right support (and medication if suitable), those living with this illness can achieve and pursue what is right for them. Most of all, they can find peace, happiness and stability."

Poetry by Mark O. Decker

SUICIDE

Days spent in waiting;
Nights without a home;
Somewhere there is freedom
From this broad,
intolerable loan.
My father gave it to me;
His father, to him;
We cannot escape our nature;
Thus, we cannot win.

ABOUT THE POEM
"I wrote this poem in 1977 having had thoughts of suicide and basically the poem communicates that it's just going to be 'part of my DNA', so to speak. So, I accept that and am not afraid to face it if it comes knocking on my door. I started writing poetry in college, in my late teens, and I believe having poetry as an outlet to express my thoughts, feelings, love, anger, hate, etc. could have been a life saving tool, because I am very feelings oriented and care about things I can do nothing about. I have written a lot of poems about how much pain is in the world. The pain I see, and feel, is overwhelming sometimes. Having the ability to write about it, express it, expunge it, has been a great gift."

GRANDPA KILLED HIMSELF

Grandpa died a lonely death;
A stark and cruel end
for a man who gave up all hope;
But, why?
Was it Aunt Deborah's death?
Was he having a mortal affair?
Why would Grandpa kill himself
and forever punish those around him;
To shoot yourself through the heart
tells a woeful tale;
God forgive his soul;
God help us all;
Self-destruction is a sin
we carry for generations;

God help us all;
Suicide is not painless;
It's brainless and torture;
A coward's way out;
Amen.

ABOUT THE POEM
"I am being judgmental here; when I wrote this poem I was struggling to figure out what would possess my grandfather - with a wife, a son and two daughters living at home - to take his life. And the family didn't discuss it, so it was just always an elephant in the room when my Aunt's would visit, or if the subject somehow came up. I can see, now, at 74 years-old, how my Dad must have struggled emotionally, and every other way, to come to grips with this family tragedy."

ROYAL BURRIS DECKER

My Grandpapa Decker took his own life
in the basement of his home
in a most unpleasant way;
I know who found him,
and the gun;
It was on Halloween in 1937,
Just a year and a half since
his beloved Deborah passed so young;
I'd like to know, but never will ...

Did he speak of why?
Did he leave a note?
I guess he didn't believe in heaven;
Suicide is not painless,
not for those who must live on
through the fog and haze
left behind;

Left for his son and daughters
with shame and anger;
How does one just wake up one day
and say to himself,
there is no tomorrow?

Young Bud wept, as did NaNaw;
And that was that.

WHAT GRANDPA DECKER SAID

No one ever talked about my grandpa,
Royal Burris Decker;
All I knew was he drilled oil wells,
and died on Halloween, in 1937;
Was I shocked to find out how he died?
I was shocked, and I was a teenager when I heard;
My mother told me, in 1989, that before killing himself,
in his basement, he left a suicide note;
My grandmother showed my mom the note;
He called my Grandmother a "Madonna",
and he asked my Dad to take the two girls,
his sisters, Martha & Minnie Louise,
out west to start a new life drilling for oil;
The note ended with squiggly, unreadable, unintelligible lines;
Sadness, inside of sadness, inside of sadness;
Family stigma, fear, staring at the great abyss;
My grandpa's house was sold on the courthouse steps in a sheriff's sale;
Thanks Dad and Mom, for rebuilding our, your lives, on solid ground;
Who will ever know how you did it.

ABOUT THE POEMS
"I'm putting a name on the suicide now - my Grandfather's name - and looking at suicide at arm's length, as if it were a stranger, someone, not family I was writing about. Of course, he was a complete stranger to me. I never met him, and have almost nothing of his that would make it a deeply personal connection - other than, of course, my amazing Dad. Being judgmental again, but grasping to know, wanting to know; Why? What was going on in his life that caused him to believe he, and those he loved and who loved him, would be better off without him in the world."

ABOUT MARK
Mark is based the USA, and has been writing poetry all his adult life. When he retired in 2016, he organized his poetry chronologically, and began self-publishing his poetry in books. He and his bride, Molly, are celebrating their 50th anniversary in 2023. They have been blessed with three children and ten grandchildren.
E: mdeckersr@gmail.com
Instagram: @okeypoet

Interview with Dustin Pickering
By Ken Jones

Diagnosed with schizoaffective bipolar, Dustin's traumatic childhood of neglect and abuse has made him the wounded person he is today. But through this, he found art and literature, and deeper ways of knowing himself.

Hi Dustin. You and I have worked together for many years on poetry publications and performances, but until your recent interview with 'Borderless' (reprinted in 'Countercurrents') I wasn't as aware of the impact mental health issues have had on your life and work. Can you briefly explain what mental health issues you face or have faced in the past?
I was diagnosed with ADHD as a young boy. That diagnosis swung into bipolar in my teens. In my early 20's I was finally diagnosed with schizoaffective bipolar type which seems a suitable diagnosis.

Growing up, I was a restless kid. Red food colouring made me hyperactive. I took Ritalin which made me delusional. I even went through a study so the physicians could see my brain waves in sleep to determine what may be wrong. I had a difficult and traumatic childhood which include permanent separation from my biological parents. This started me off on the wrong foot. When my illness reached full swing, it terrified me. I talked to a being who changed personalities multiple times. At first he was a bully I knew in junior high. He told me the woman I adored at the time was his soulmate. I ended up destroying my lovely acoustic guitar. Then he became my father who was friendly and loving to me. Later, he was Satan and the delusions kicked in at that point. They snuck up on me in college, and I had to drop out due to them and depression. Depression made concentrating and focus impossible. During the worst of the delusional period, my grandmother told me I looked very sick. I was pale. I hadn't slept well and was scared of what the voices told me. They told me I had signed contracts with Satan, that caused the entire world to go to hell and only I could save the world. I would be tortured myself in eternity for messing with the spiritual world - one I hadn't even believed in because I was an atheist.

At a bus stop on the way home from Mississippi, a young man stopped me and asked if I was feeling OK. He said I looked "very sick." My grandmother told me to look at myself. I literally looked like Marilyn Manson. Dark eyes, pale face. I remember it well. I spent that period praying on command of this voice to save the world. It would tell me to pray in random places at random times. Including at that bus stop, in the cafeteria, in a crowd of people. Today, the mood issues are problematic. Delusions are not a problem because of the medications. I am living on disability with a modest check from the government. I work on occasion for extra money and to get out of the house.

Mental health issues often run in families both through genetics and environment. Can you talk about your family history in this regard?
I have a cousin with schizophrenia who I don't know personally. My dad may be bipolar. I was told my mother was schizophrenic, but she told me herself she only has anxiety and depression. My parents met in a psychiatric unit. My dad was undersocialized. The family quickly fizzled out when my mother's mother was violently killed by a drunk driver when I was two. I don't remember any of this but I've been told.

My mother went into a long spell of grief and according to her my father was not supportive enough. They had financial troubles as well. Eventually my mom left for another man when they agreed on divorce. I would not see her again until I was 30 years old. My maternal grandmother is said to have had a dream two weeks before she died. She was holding me in her arms and a dark mysterious force robbed her of me and she couldn't do anything about it. After my parents' separation, I was placed with my paternal grandmother and his sister for care. They raised me. He was required to pay child support, which he did not. Later, they allowed me to live with him on two separate occasions. Both times his new wife was physically and emotionally abusive to me. His sister sent tuition money to pay for my schooling, and yet my tuition was never paid. Discipline was not even handed between me and my brothers, who were children at the time. I was blamed for everything and not given lunch money to eat. I charged my lunch to the school, until they would no longer allow me to do so. She also hit me and left bruises. After seeing marks on my face, a teacher asked me what happened. I told her my stepmom had aggressively clawed me with her nails that morning. She suggested I call CPS. It was also said I would not do well in life because of the abuse and my peers' general rejection of me. I've been the victim of bullying since I can remember. It was difficult and still hurts to think on how I was treated during that period (12 years-old). Both my stepmom and dad deny this ever took place, but I remember it clearly. During two suicide attempts forced on me by my delusions, my aunt was the only person who could be there for me. One morning I woke up in a hospital after OD'ing on sleeping pills, and I kept having seizures. They pumped my stomach. I fell asleep. When I woke up, my aunt was holding my hand. When I raised up, I would suddenly shoot back down and go into seizures. She would squeeze my hand to make sure I was OK. All this during a work day! After she had to leave, I finally relaxed. She stood by me the entire time to make sure I was safe. As a little boy I actually drowned in a swimming pool and she resuscitated me. I literally owe her my life.

Current research indicates many mental health issues are based in physiological factors, particularly brain chemistry. Has that research impacted your views on the impact of mental health issues on your life and on any treatment you receive?
I take two medications for psychosis and mood swings, as well as one for side effects. I hope one day to see genetic treatments that are able to repair such problems at their source. I have a pet interest in neurology because I want to understand the human brain. I discovered myself that depression has serious physiological consequences and is not just a mood problem. It is physically painful. I personally apply behavioural cognitive approaches to myself. I learned about them from one of my previous psychiatrists.

Traditional talk therapy is often recommended to purge psychological problems and/or trauma. I sometimes joke with my friends that "my poetry is my therapy". Have you been through talk therapy? Do you believe your work serves a similar function?
I saw a psychologist as a child, but have not since. I agree that art is therapeutic but I also think there are deeper dimensions of personal discovery and adventure in art. I find it reassuring and healing to write and do the other artistic pursuits I commit to. It helps me stay focused, realize who I am, and think deeper on life. I think it was my paternal grandmother who encouraged my interest in the arts and literature. She had a vast collection of books and loved van Gogh.

How does your psychological and family history have impacted your work?
I know I have an entire poetry manuscript based on my childhood trauma that I've pledged to shelve until my Mother passes away.

Do you have any specific work that addresses the impact mental health issues have on your own or your family's behaviour or ultimately the way you or they have lived life?
I think without all the family history I certainly would not be the wounded person I am, and wounds require healing. Those wounds dragged me deeper into myself, to think on things in ways I was not taught. Combined with a higher intelligence than average, it pushed

me to reflect on things and also to become more understanding of people. I've had some fantastic friends who have shown me things outside my scope as well, and I've been willing to listen. I have several memoir pieces that may one day be published. However, I am silent on many things out of respect for the parties involved as I think they are well- intentioned just not equipped to handle the situations that faced them.

POSSIBILITY'S COINCIDENCE

Star —
the cylinder birth of cavernous Earth
disappointed
Fantasmal origin, god of cyclical
brooding, recompense.
I hear the music through the wall.
Judgment of the past, forms present
part of the future
Helen deep in love with the fruits of
discord.
Panthers slowly trickle from the future
to the realm of boredom, present.
Sets fire to adulterated fun, lack
of enthusiasm for.
The present is popcorn —
always lifting its boredom on high,
exalting.
The past is always popping corn.
Hearting the string.
The floods of tempestuous flame acknowledge
no saviour.
We are secretly burning the forbidden
letters of yesterday.
Tomorrow's leeches are shallow tide prophets
whistling on the wind.
As the present sits in the middle, weighing
possibility.

THE BALCONY

I saw you on the balcony,
waving toward the threshold
of dark oblivion.

Curtains dangling overhead,
sweet lustre in the air:
a vanishing question, silent.

I finally spin to see her dancing,
dancing on the stair.
Then I face the never-ending doorway of doom.

ABOUT DUSTIN
Diagnosed with schizoaffective bipolar, Dustin's traumatic childhood of neglect and abuse has made him the wounded person he is today. But through this, he found art and literature, and deeper ways of knowing himself.
FB: @pickering.dustin

ABOUT KEN
Ken Jones is a native Texan who has published ten full length poetry collections, numerous chapbooks, and hundreds of individual poems in literary journals, anthologies, websites and other forums, as well as performing his original work for over 30 years as a Featured Poet at bookstores, conferences, festivals, and countless venues in Texas and across the United States.
E: poetken@yahoo.com

Prose by Sheila A. Donovan

THEY'LL BE SORRY

Making people be sorry was the last thing on my mind that day. I doubt it's anyone's last thought as they ponder suicide.

I lost a job in a 17-year career with the airlines when it closed the local office. I'd earned awards for being top seller. I had traveled to five continents and met many people. I stayed in touch with them. Now I was jobless, unemployed; I lost my identity.

I decided to go into real estate. It was a struggle. Had to purchase a car. I depended on my severance pay to get the car's down payment and to pay my mortgage. There was no income for months. I tried for two years to make a living. Sold my jewelry to hang on. Lived on ramen soup and peanut butter sandwiches. Managed to pay my mortgage but fell behind on condo assessments.

My real estate career had major problems. I had a buyer threaten to sue me because the empty building I'd sold had horses that had snuck in there between contract and closing. Yes, in Chicago! The buyer, a lawyer, falsely claimed I knew about the horses. Gave up my commission to avoid a lawsuit. Sold a major commercial space, and the day before closing the seller backed out. I had a ready, willing, and able buyer contracted. The sellers knew I'd sue them, but it would take two years to go to court. With sparse income, I had to sell my car and leave real estate. I won the case when it was finally tried, but by then I'd relinquished my real estate license.

My age made companies hesitate to hire me. I worked in retail and as a babysitter for minimum wage to hold me over until I could get a better-paying job.

I no longer could afford to socialize. Couldn't go to the movies, dinners, or events with friends. Didn't want my family to know I was a failure. Each time I started to call someone to get together with them I thought "They'll only say no," and I didn't make the call. Feeling that I was a burden to everyone, I stopped contact. Fearful and depressed I turned inwards.

The day of my attempted suicide I curled into a ball on my living room floor, rocking and crying. Hopelessness overtook my brain and heart. I swallowed an entire jar of antidepressants. Lying on the floor, waiting for the release of death, I argued with myself: "Maybe it's not hopeless. No, it's too late. The medicine is already messing up my brain. I don't want to live with brain damage."

"NO, IT'S NOT TOO LATE. GET UP!" I convinced myself.

I dressed quickly and hopped a cab to the hospital's

emergency room. I told him to hurry because it was an emergency. He slowly eased to a stop at each stop sign. Didn't drive around other cars. Repeating "This is an emergency!" I told him to drive faster. It didn't faze him. He poked along all the way to the emergency room four miles away. I didn't want to admit to him that I'd attempted suicide. Maybe that would have made him take it seriously and drive faster.

The doctors on duty interviewed me. Soon they forced a charcoal drink down my throat. I tried not to gag. Several hours later, feeling wiped out and weak from vomiting, they dismissed me. Since I was uninsured, they were sending me to a public mental hospital. I begged them not to. "I won't do it again. Really!"

They shipped me off in a black limousine with a uniformed driver.

The driver was psychologically sicker than any patient he'd transported. He started laughing, mocking me. He yelled "You're a loser. I'm taking you to the funny farm. Nobody wants you. They're gonna lock you up." I was terrified of this man. It was just me and him in the middle of the night, what was there to stop him from raping me? (I'd been raped about 7 years previously.) Getting up my nerve I stated "I'm going to report you when we get to the hospital." His reply, cackling. "Who are they gonna believe, ME or you - the crazy person?"

Upon arrival, I was checked in. Didn't mention the driver, knowing they wouldn't believe me. Then I witnessed what a hellhole this place was.

As I was being interviewed, a harried nurse tried to force me to take medicine. I declared, "I just came from having my stomach pumped, ejecting all the pills I've swallowed. I'm NOT taking any more pills." Thankfully, she stopped. Exhausted, I was told "You cannot go to bed now. It's still being used." Unbelievable that beds had to be scheduled, limited to certain hours. Were they serious?

Exhausted, I slumped like an unstuffed rag doll on a chair until I could go to bed an hour later.

The hospital staff kept everyone doped up. It was frightening being among these patients knowing that I was one of them. I was merely depressed, not insane. Some were schizophrenic or psychotic.

This place was a living horror story.

They had me join a group therapy session. It was eye opening! So many people who were physically, mentally or sexually abused by parents or other adults when they were young.

I was allowed one call, so I dialled one of my sisters to rescue me from that pit. She was instructed that she must take me to another hospital's mental ward. I ended up in a decent hospital, close to where my siblings lived in the suburbs. It was clean and had much better conditions.

They made me stop taking Xanax cold turkey. My cholesterol was dangerously low too, which causes depression and anxiety. Luckily, I did not suffer any withdrawal effects. Could the side effects of Xanax have led me to attempt suicide?

I was allowed to leave the hospital grounds to walk around the block. So empowering. They didn't treat me as dangerous.

My psychologist was horrendous. She was a war victim who compared everything that she'd gone through to what I revealed in sessions. Whatever I mentioned, she would reply; "You didn't have it so bad. We had to dig into frozen ground to find potatoes to eat." She negated my problems, frustrating me. I know that professionals are not supposed to tell you their troubles in counseling.

I was released after one week there; "cured". It was because I was unemployed and uninsured. They knew the odds of collecting extended- stay payments were thin.

I got further counseling from sessions with a Social Worker in my neighborhood. He was caring, a great listener, and had me draw pictures of the most traumatic issues in my life. We discussed the problems. He released me from feeling worthless and hopeless.

He convinced me that life was worth living again.

Thank you, Jim!

ABOUT SHEILA
Based in Chicago, USA, Sheila was first published at age 15. She has poems in numerous issues of the following anthologies: *Reflections Journal, Poetry Cram, Journal of Modern Poetry, Dear Mr. President, The Ultimate Chicago Poetry Anthology, You Don't Know Us*, and *Love, Death, and Everything in Between*. Sheila also was published in *PSA Magazine*, and the newspapers *Skyline* and *Chicago Journal*. She earned Best of Show at the Bucktown Arts Fest, for her children's Poet-Tea session, and the Contemporary American Poetry Prize Honorable Mention for her poem *Universal Failure*. Sheila has been a judge at Louder Than a Bomb. She volunteered for eight years at Open Books, teaching kids how to write slam poetry. Sheila devoted thirty years to volunteer tutoring at Off The Street Club. Her poems have been exhibited at Woman Made Gallery. She's been the featured poet at numerous venues around Chicago, including Beach Poets and the Harold Washington Library. A short, romantic story from Sheila is about to be published in a national magazine, and she has poems and essays in the Budlong Woods upcoming anthology. She thanks her grandfather for reading poetry to her in his Irish brogue which whet her creativity.
E: sheilaAdonovanwriter@gmail.com

Poetry by Sheryl L. Fuller

UNDENIABLE SORROW

Undeniable sorrow
With no promise of tomorrow
How can we begin
To see the pain that lived within
A castaway, a lost soul
Led astray with no place to go

Denial of societies glance
To rise above the noise and dance
Turned away from everything
No where to run, no voice to sing

A forgotten shadow to the world, left behind in silent pain
Spinning in an infinite swirl, of the same thoughts over and over again
When peace evaded you, no place was safe
Those lies were not true, for you; a gentle careless waif

Why didn't you shut out the voices, why didn't you decide to change
Didn't you know you had choices, to sing and dance again
Where did the time go, The times you used to laugh
Where was the world, Offering you a second chance

Small town or big where you would roam
Seeking a friend to help you live
Any delicate place to call a home
Anywhere with some love to give

For a moment I thought I saw you, I see you everywhere
I thought I heard you call my name; those thoughts are often near
In my undeniable sorrow, I never said good-bye
With no promise of tomorrow, all I can do is cry

ABOUT SHERYL
Sheryl is an author, poet, musician, and singer songwriter from Chicago, USA. Her writing is inspired by the people she has met and the places she has been. She says; *"Spread love everywhere. The smallest gesture of kindness can mean the world to somebody."*
E: playnicekids@comcast.net

Poetry by Suzanne S. Eaton

CHOOSE TO STAY
(trying to talk to a child that's slipping away)

I know that something is terribly wrong,
and I reach out to you.
I see the pain in your eyes, but your words won't
come. How can I help?
Life keeps us so busy there's never time to talk about
what's actually happening inside ourselves.
I give you a pep talk and send you on your way.
I reach out to you again, but you are sullen
and withdrawn—perhaps not now.
"Talk to me when you are ready" is all I can think to say.
I feel you leaning away—oh child—please stay.

How can I reunite you with the carefree child inside
that loved life and couldn't wait to take on the world?
How can I give you perspective about
the injustice and the ugly side of this place?
I try to hug you but feel your
self-loathing holding you apart—please,
my darling, feel my heart. How can I lift
the dark ambiance trapping your soul and help
you come back to that place where it's not so hard
to shield against the meanness of others?
I see you looking away—oh, my precious child, please stay.

I saw a note you threw away and read
the names they call you. What kind of human
ignores the pain of others—causes this kind of suffering?
Where are your friends, your safety net?
Does anyone see you and offer support?
You shake and cry as I inquire and close off even more.
I'll find someone more skilled than I—for you
to talk to—will you try?
I know it seems so hopeless, so draining—so terminal.
I hear you ask how you can begin again
when all you want is the pain to end.
But please—my baby, choose to stay.

The cruelty of this life is only part of the experience.

In time, it fades. We can move away from whatever
it is and find a place for our reality to
be free and fully realized. Or just a place to rest.
You are safe with me. You are the center of my
world; I can never be ok if you choose to end your stay.
I'll help you see the incredible person inside
that has no reason to hide. I'll help you
find hope. The years ahead will be kinder, I promise.
We will laugh again. Still, I see you pulling away.
God help me! Is there anything at all I can say?
I need you here—please, please, please stay!

Let tomorrow be another day.

ABOUT THE POEM
"'Chose to Stay' is a poem I wrote reflecting on a son who spoke of giving up, and worried us for a few years, and when my granddaughter tried to end her life, and all that her mother and I shared about our feeling in that helpless situation."

TONIGHT'S INTERVENTION

Sleep escapes me again tonight.
I close my eyes, and suddenly, I am filled

with bedim images that make me wheeze and quiver
—there is no peace, no might to compose myself.

In the shadows, the demon of shame
slinks and creeps to horrify my soul.

I cannot rest an instant, or I will lose
what's left of my mind—that I yet control.

A damp mist of evil sweeps the room
and begins to rise from floor to ceiling,

air is thick and somehow burns my skin.
A vapor prevails and fills my face

to block my starving view. I gasp!

Vexing dark eyes stark and steady—over there,

staring, glaring, piercing through
the blackest black.

Defecting in my weakness,
I fight to breathe but find no air.

Diabolical devilry fills the space,
besieges, traps, petrifies, and holds,

shrouding me with a noxious sense of depravity.
I melt into my sodden bed,

not able to move—breathing turns to shallow pants
my heart beats wildly in my ears,

harsh and hateful blasts of rancor gnaw and bite,
consume me piece by piece.

My soul bleeds out like venom.
I see myself with rabid scorn and odious awe.

Enough! I search my soul—force my mind
to flash upon His face—a seed of hope!

I hold the image tightly and lock upon
the slightest beam of light that

begins to pierce the darkness.
I magnetize my mind to draw and expand

the only panacea that can
blast out the heresy of this state.

Light's embrace proliferates,
shadows groan as they're vigorously displaced.

All at once, the shifting room is calm
My bed is still, the air is clear.

Evil shrinks, no eyes, no glare,
the mist expunged, I can breathe again.

In bright light, I think of Him,
the love He has for me—how capable,

how strong I feel—His warm light rushes in.
There is no dominion strong enough

to stay His loving intervention.
My faith restored, I face the night again.

First published in *Poet's Choice Anthology* March, '21.

ABOUT THE POEM
"'Tonight's Intervention' was written from personal experience; many nights I went through this process and held on to the light of Christ with all my might."

EVEN TO THE TREE

You're like this leaf, my child
fallen golden now.
Once you were green.

You shimmered in the
dewdrops of your faith.
What powerful gust,
what wind's persuasion
has swept you from the tree
--has sent you swirling aimlessly
with all the others?

Are you doomed to drift and crumble,
never again to see the life-giving branch?

Oh, quickly, grasp the memory of your faith,
reach up to that sweet Savior
who lived and died for you, for me,
that miracles might return a leaf
--even to the tree.

You're like this leaf, my child
fallen golden now.
Once you were green.

First published in *FAITH*, April, '21.

ABOUT THE POEM
"'Even to the Tree' was written with great angst over my daughter."

THE ERROR OF MY WAYS

Come to me, spirit much greater than I.
Give light to my mind and softness to my heart.
Hear me breathing, see the bleeding of my soul.
Show me how to take tomorrow and with it change.
Shield me from the cruelty of things
that have no place with you.
Revive me in my quest. Give me rest.
I am without strength to go on.
I don't know where to turn or what to do
to solve the cosmic problems that attack me.
Please, please, please, heal my heart
and lift my burdens a touch.
Let me know you're there--that you care.
Give me just one small prompt that I may take
another step and not fear that it's in error.

First published in *Poet's Choice Anthology* December, '22.

ABOUT THE POEM
"'The Error of My Ways' is a poem I wrote in a period of deep depression as I tried to find hope and connection with a higher power."

THE LAST LIE

Gray clouds erupt in soft blue space.
      rain—surging with the end of day,
     wind—cold against my neck and face,
a brutal storm is on its way.

I hear you coming breath by breath,
    I freeze in static desperation
        trapped in life but edging death
drenched in breathless expectation.

Splashing skies and shadows new
        a gash of light shows you're not there,
        with wounded eyes, I search for you
—not here—not now—not anywhere.

Blackening funnels spin and pound
        rain beats on me right where I lay
        against my face—the soaking ground
shivering anguish begs to wash away.

ABOUT THE POEM
"*'The Last Lie' is a poem I wrote about a person I loved who took her own life after being stood up one to many times by someone she loved.*"

ABOUT ALL THE POEMS
"*Suicide; I have struggled with this ideation and have had a son, a daughter, and a granddaughter at very high risk, and have worked hard to keep them in life with us. My ex-husband also tried to end his life on more than one occasion. It is heartbreaking from every perspective.*"

ABOUT SUZANNE
Suzanne is an author and marketing consultant. She shares her "soul carvings" that speak of love, loss, and family with great joy. Most recently, *Writer Shed Stories, Seaborne Magazine, Scars Publications, The Purpled Nail, The Silent World in Her Vase, Scarlet Leaf Review, Rue Scribe, eris & eros, Writing in a Woman's Voice, The Elevation Review, The Write Launch, Dreamers, Poet's Choice (11), Carmina Magazine, Wingless Dreamer, Unlimited787Literature, Literary Excellence/Ariel's Dream, Free Spirit (4), Dewdrop,* and *Beyond Words* have selected her work for publication. Suzanne is a contributing author to the book *Making Peace with Your Pieces*, and the WINNER of Wingless Dreamer's Memories Contest.
FB: @zan.eaton.5
Instagram: @eaton9191
Twitter: @SuzanneSEaton7

Poetry by Gary Shulman, MS. Ed.

FOR MAURY
(Honoring a young man who left this world too early)

Sometimes in life an angel appears
So fragile yet profoundly strong
So much to live for
A bright light in the storm
So how could it go so wrong?
Contemplate as you will
Of reasons, how comes, and whys
It truly is all in vain
You'll never quite understand those whys
Nor his never-ending pain
Let us just celebrate his peaceful legacy
His smile, his laughter his sweet gentility
And never let another lost soul
So deep in unrelenting pain
EVER leave this corporeal world thinking his life was just in vain
A life cut short is tragedy
A life cut short has no reason nor a rhyme
From another dimension dear Maury lives
In our hearts, minds and souls everlasting for all time

ABOUT THE POEM
As a retired professional in the field of support services for vulnerable families caring for children with disabilities, I have been privileged to meet other dedicated professionals in the field. Sometimes they have they own personal demons that haunt them as they support others in need. One such individual was a young man by the name of Maury. Sadly, his demons tormented him to the point that he chose to end his pain while only in his early 20s. My poem is dedicate to him."

ABOUT GARY
Based in California, USA, Gary has spent a lifetime supporting vulnerable families and children. He began his career working with children with and without disabilities in an inclusive Head Start program in Brooklyn, New York. He then transitioned to become the Special Needs and Early Childhood Coordinator for the Brooklyn Children's Museum for ten years. His passion for advocacy grew as he worked more and more with parents of children with disabilities. For over 24 years he passionately advocated for the needs of these parents as the Social Services and Training Director for Resources for

Children with Special Needs, Inc. in NYC. The last eight years of his working life, Gary served as a private Special Needs Consultant, conducting hundreds of training sessions throughout NYC, and beyond, to help parents and professionals find and access the services and systems required to facilitate maximizing the potential of their children with disabilities. Now happily retired, he still volunteers his time any way he can to provide information to those in need of his expertise.
E: shulman.gary@yahoo.com
W: www.garyshulman.jimdo.com

Poetry by Douglas Colston

VALĒ GRANDMA

To begin at the beginning involves speaking of a loving husband and wife
who had some children and a long marriage that ended in widowhood –
the type of widowhood that unintentionally resulted in the added shock
of disempowerment and social isolation …
the latter exacerbated by simmering conflicts with children.

A pattern of intergenerational religious intolerance is a poisoned chalice
and when one daughter marries into the 'offending' faith
seeds of discord will usually find fertile ground in many minds –
and this fractured one mother-daughter relationship here.

Mother-son relationships were also fraught for a variety of reasons
including those arising from the psychological difficulties encountered
by one son dealing with terminal congenital illnesses
experienced by his first wife and their daughter –
his actions were understandable, imperfect and barely tolerated …
and the younger son lived at a distance (emotionally and physically).

The youngest daughter remained her mother's champion –
even as her own marriage was disintegrating
as a consequence of her husband's unrelenting infidelities
and the domestic violence that followed –
including making arrangements for her mother to relocate
and cohabitate with her and her children.

Another complicating factor was the treatment of the relevant Depression
(for both the mother and daughter)
in the form of Mogadon and Valium –
a mind-addling combination of drugs that affected many in the 1970s.

Part two of the story might be when a grandson was sent to wake his Grandma –
she had apparently slept in –
only to find her unresponsive and overdosed …

that chapter ended with the 'sensible' decision,
mediated by the abusive husband,
for the widow to return to her own home.

In time that grandson accompanied his mother to his Grandma's house
to check on her welfare after telephone calls remained unanswered over a few day –
his mother discovered her own mother had suicided …
fortunately sparing her teenage son that task,
although she did share the details
and left him to deal with the Ambos when they arrived.

That grandson loved his grandmother
and mourned her loss
and the psychological impacts experienced by his own mother,
but he understood what was involved …
at least enough to harbor no ill-will,
to allow his grief to resolve in an adaptive manner
and to be supportive of those who expressed their own unresolved grief
(of one form or another).

Even when presented with his youngest uncle's
drunken solipsistic rant
of how he would never forgive his mother for letting his sister discover her suicide,
he didn't say,

"The rest of you are really responsible –
you left her with the task
because you all abandoned your own mother".

Instead, he said,

"Mum understood what I did –
that Grandma was terribly depressed after Grandpa's death,
she never recovered
and the anti-depressants she was treated with
caused disastrous cognitive problems for her –
and she held none of that,
or the circumstances of that day,
against Grandma …
in the circumstances,
if she didn't identify an unforgivable transgression,

there probably isn't one to find".

That uncle subsequently defrauded that grandson's inheritance –
intergenerational and personal trauma can manifest in all sorts of ways –
but the end of this story is yet to be written …
only time will tell
how future generations will be affected by that suicide
(hopefully 'love', 'understanding' and 'compassion' will prevail).

ABOUT THE POEM
"'*Valē Grandma*' *captures incidents and themes that I have discussed (occasionally) with my wife and children. My intentions in writing it today are the same as much - if not all - of my writing: to make a positive contribution to the zeitgeist. As the events unfolded and as they are recounted, it serves as an example of how loving rational thinking can operationalised as a guiding principle even in the most challenging circumstances.*"

ABOUT DOUG
Douglas hails from Australia, has played in Ska bands and picked up university degrees, supported his parents during terminal illnesses, developed chronic mental and physical illnesses pursuant to sustained workplace harassment, married his love, fathered two great children, had his inheritance embezzled and, among other things, he is pursuing a Ph.D he hopes will provide a positive contribution to the zeitgeist. In addition to appearing in a number of collections, his fiction, non-fiction and poetry has appeared in various anthologies and magazines including: *POETiCA REViEW; I, mpspired, New Note Poetry, Rue Scribe, Inlandia: A Literary Journey,* and *Revue {R}évolution.*
W: www.theancientoracle.com
FB: @douglas.colston

Poetry by John Gallas

GREYMOUTH SONNET
"The drowning man is not troubled by rain" – Iraqi proverb.

The pleasure-boat that gave me none has passed.
Its bright propellors' bubbled swirl withdraws
with fitful beat. The deep, like two closed doors,
is dark and bars the upward way. At last,
reversed in every blue desire to rise,
I sink more surely down than I had heart
to dare for. They are gone now. Shall I start,
so late, the selfish struggle to be wise?
Not now – when far above I hear the rain,
whose distant whisper worries me no more,
like wind on someone else's roof. What for?
The tender blue turns black and drowns my pain.

The last-loosed bubble leaves me: jelly-bright,
it falls in hurried hope towards the light.

ABOUT JOHN
John is a New Zealand poet. Books include: *The Song Atlas, The Extasie, The Little Sublime Comedy, The Gnawing Flood* and *17 Paper Resurrections.*
W: www.johngallaspoetry.co.uk

Poetry by Karla Linn Merrifield

MY THREE SUICIDES

Her last few years were deeply unhappy ones: Martha.
His last few years were deeply angry ones: Jimmy.
His last few years were deeply painful ones: Beau.

Couldn't write himself out of advanced diabetes, poor Beau.
Couldn't paint herself out of menopausal depression, poor Martha.
Couldn't sing himself out of cirrhosis of the liver, poor Jimmy.

Thus left for little sister: bonedust, Jimmy's;
thus left for fellow poets: a great heart, Beau's;
thus left for son of sons: a soul entire, Martha's;

and Burchfield, Merrifield and Cutts became once upon a time.

COLLATERAL DAMAGE

JoJo, erstwhile Pollyanna poet, expected
his crime to be victimless, but a handgun,
bullets loaded, came into play, so, shit no,
shit out of luck, no such line to twist;
imagination's muse committed suicide thinking
he'd not hurt anybody but himself. Like shit.
Inspiration went bang, splat, and JoJo began
making broken breaks in his name—
poems born lame of syllable, crippled of word.

RHETORICAL SUICIDE
with words from Percy Bysshe Shelley

His poems were *ghosts from an encounter*
fleeing in eerie combinations of anaphora and
epistrophe resulting in simple symploce

His words desired to open neighboring clauses.
His words craved beginnings.
His words lusted for the fresh start.

But far outside his native trope in the end,

he became a simulacrum of beauty in the end.
He fired once, flash, bang, specter in the end.

In the beginning was his end.
In the beginning was his end.
In the beginning was his end.

You simply disappear in the afterlife of symploce.

First appeared in *The Weekly Avocet*, January 2014

THE NINE THINGS YOU DON'T KNOW ABOUT ME

are subsumed under the first: a pistol hole
may indeed hold the wild, wide whole
fuckin' world, should be headline news wholly
top-story news, science news, whole-
some weed news, for tonight in the night sky, holy
Orion wields the whole
enchilada—belt, sword—whole-
heartedly in a whole-
sale, self-inflicted blow out by bullet hole
is the headless Hunter's dead stars' finale of holiness

ABOUT THE POEMS
"These poems were written in response to the shocking, violent suicide of one of my dearest lifelong friends; a poet and world sailor who physical deterioration from multiple diseases prompted him to take his own life rather than continue to live in constant pain and physical deteriorations. He shot himself in the chest in his bathroom shower stall. Writing the poems helped me process the shocking news and the profound loss."

ABOUT KARLA
Karla bases herself between New York and Florida, USA. She has had over 1000 poems published journals and anthologies worldwide, and has 16 books to her credit. Following her 2018 *Psyche's Scroll* (Poetry Box Select) is the full-length book *Athabaskan Fractal: Poems of the Far North* (Cirque Press). She is also a frequent contributor to The Songs of *Eretz Poetry Review*. Her newest poetry collection, *My Body the Guitar* - nominated for the 2022 National Book Award - was inspired by famous guitarists and their guitars.
W: www.karlalinnmerrifield.org
Twitter: @LinnMerrifiel

Poetry by Sanda Ristić-Stojanović

DO NOT KILL YOURSELF
(Translation Sonja Asanović Todorović)

Don't kill yourself
your heart is the core and architecture of existence,
your words educate these shores between which
we all swim like the life of life.

I am standing on the street, your existence is becoming the best man
with confessions of my mirrors.
The Cluster of the Moon trenches into our collective surrealism.

Your heart is a fantasy of shadows,
but the shadows persistent to pronounce life,
your footsteps feel the songs of existence and
a song of existence they give to me.
Your words flow into the clairvoyance of the stars and the infidelity of history and
they defend the heart of our grown times.
The architectures of anxiety and love forgive your architectures.

The craziness of the Sun loves us,
the licentiousness of the heart of the night and the heart of the day
borrows everything from us.
I am a general, a beggar, a love, a friend, an anxiety, a prophet,
life, soldier, father, son, mother - of this time and
I'm telling you, don't kill yourself.

ABOUT THE POEM
"I worked in two secondary schools in Belgrade for about 15 years as a teacher of philosophy, logic and civics. In that period, two of my students committed suicide — the girl Janja T. (16) and the young man Alexsander V. (1991-2010). I remember that class in Alexander's 4/8 class, and the last conversation with Alexander. He was extremely nervous. The topic was Progress, and for something I said at one point he said: it's pointless. After that class, I had a feeling of disappointment and exhaustion. Three or four days later Alexsander hanged himself from the chandelier of his house, which was the subject of a dispute in his parents' divorce case. I regret that all of us teachers did not recognize his mental state and his cry for help. On the day when the news came that Alexsander had committed suicide, about twenty of us staff cried in the school hall.

The professor of sociology told me; Sanda, we have 1000 students, it happens, it just does. I answered him - both as a poet and as a professor of philosophy - that should not have happened. After that tragic incident, I introduced occasional classes where I would talk to the students about all the topics that concern their lives and youth. Once I came to a class and said to the students - today you are doing a test in philosophy. Then I saw a girl crying in the back bench. I told her to come to me and tell me quietly what was going on. She told me quite a serious reason. That's when I made a decision - everyone is taking the test except for the girl who was crying. I said to my student who was crying - you will sit next to me at the desk, we will talk to the whole class. After that class, I included the school psychologist to help my student."

ABOUT SANDA

Sanda lives in Serbia, and graduated in philosophy at the Belgrade Faculty of Philosophy. She is the author of 15 poetry books, and one of four authors in the joint collection of poems, *From the Shadow of the Verse* (Gramatik, 2012). She was an editor in the publishing house Beletra, editor-in-chief of the literary magazine *Kovina* (KOV, Vršac), and her poems and short stories have been published in numerous anthologies and collections of contemporary literature. She is a member of the Serbian Literary Society, the Association of Serbian Writers, and the Aesthetic Society of Serbia.

E: sandastojanovic@yahoo.com

FB: @sanda.risticstojanovic

Poetry by Bobby Z

CAN'T YOU HEAR ME KNOCKIN'

Here we go again,
knockin' on heaven's door,
may have been here,
many times before.

Knockin' on heaven's door,
will I ever be admitted,
misdeeds from the past,
will I ever be acquitted.

The thought of remembering,
the memories of yesteryear's,
can't you hear me knockin',
while I wipe away the tears.

Do you hear me knockin',
have I forever been banished,
not born with a silver spoon,
for this will I forever be punished.

Time slowly disappearing,
revealing the fact,
that it soon may be over,
definitely the deck was stacked.

Close calls and near misses,
have always been the norm,
time is running out,
too late to reform.

Will the door always remain closed,
shall I always be viewed as a rebel,
not enough time to pay for the misdeeds,
guess I'll be dancing with the devil.

Nolo Segundo's story
The Day I Remembered My Soul

When I was 24, I killed myself. I put it that bluntly because it was not an attempted suicide, a cry for help, but a decision to self-murder. Yes, it was a desperate act, a last attempt to escape what my mind feared as lifetime imprisonment in a mental asylum [they still did that back in the early '70s]. It was even, in its own way, logical - to my then agnostic mind at least. I had been suffering a profound clinical depression—the kind where you stop eating, sleeping, emoting, desiring. In time your body begins to break down: I shook like an old man with Parkinson's instead of the once healthy and robust young man of just a few weeks earlier. I had decided as a teenager that there was no God, no soul, no heaven or hell - all just fantasies for those [unlike myself] not brave enough to accept that death means extinction of not only the body but the personality, consciousness itself. I know many people have that view today, and it does not appear to bother them, Well, why would it, until they're faced with their own deaths?

    Now what I'm about to relate will be believed by some, disbelieved by others, and the rest will probably just shrug their shoulders and give it no more thought. Yet is there really any question more important than the possibility of life after death: That you, your character, personality, memories - your consciousness will continue, not for years or decades but forever. We are the only species out of millions to have a sense of mortality—then too, we are the only transcendent species as well. And I think they are related, because what I was 'shown' [the best if rather feeble word I can come up with] is that I am two beings, sharing the same space or life as it were for a time: the one mortal, the other immortal, existing without beginning or end, beyond time itself. The mortal one we all can see, the other one is trickier—though I suspect far more people have experienced something of the 'paranormal' than one might surmise, based on accounts I have been told over the years. [Oxford did a study finding that 71% of the population had had at least one paranormal experience—and this in secular Britain.]

    I had been attending the London Film School in Covent Garden, London. I have loved movies almost as much as books since childhood. For some reason which I still do not fully understand a half century later, I dropped out in my third and final term. The unconscious mind is far more powerful than most people wish to acknowledge—can any of us really be said to know ourselves completely? Again, it's not surprising that many aren't aware they have a soul as they can't even acknowledge they have an unconscious mind which affects their thoughts and emotions, not only in their dreams but in the waking world as well.

Of course if I had thought things through, I might have decided to become a screen writer - I have wanted to become a writer since I started thinking—really thinking—as a teenager. (There too I fancied it would be writing the Great American Novel: I never thought I'd become a published poet in my 70's.) But I didn't think of it, and soon after I returned to the States I fell into a profound clinical depression, as it was termed in those days. Day after day I would walk around the dining room table in my parents house, asking myself why I had abandoned my dream—a hard thing for anyone, is it not?

Each day I walked around that table, all day long, eating less, sleeping less each night, asking myself why I had 'run away' from my one chance—as I saw it then-- to follow a childhood dream. The more I did that the more I wished I could go back in time, back to London and the film school, and stop my foolish self from 'running away'. That was part of the torment—seeking a time machine to correct my near fatal error as it turned out. My parents were not very sophisticated and thought a camping trip to Vermont with a high school buddy would 'snap me out of it'.

But each day we were driving through the beauty of that state, things just got worse. I had largely stopped sleeping or eating, my nerves were so shot my hands shook with unceasing tremors, and while I knew that the mountains and valleys we drove through were very beautiful, I did not 'feel' that beauty one iota. It was the same when I saw a pretty woman: I knew I should feel an attraction, but I felt nothing.

It got worse. One day we drove up to a scene where a dog had been hit and killed by a car, and the woman who owned it was weeping profusely. I could not understand, at all, why she was so upset. I had no empathy, I had no feelings at all it seemed, good or bad. And in subsequent years I came to realize that all our mental processes, be they thoughts/ideas, or appreciation of art and music and literature, all our human thinking is fundamentally emotional, and MUST BE BASED on an emotion - or we cease being human, alive, transcendent - and soon become the living dead.

And that is not really hyperbole. Depression does not just stop you from relating to other people, but it cuts you off from yourself as well - you feel hollow, empty, a walking shell, very much a living hell. Believing it was only going to continue to get worse until I lost complete control and was 'put away' to suffer and suffer, without hope as I saw it then, it seemed logical to end my life as soon as possible. So one night when we stopped at a large campsite by Lake Champlain, I decided that after my friend went into the tent to sleep I would walk into the lake and drown myself (for some reason I had a sense that drowning was a painless death.) But I wanted to leave my parents a good-bye note: I still had that much humanity left in me. But my hands shook so hard that the pen just made scribbles, and at that moment these words - these exact words - came into my head: 'Just let me write this'.

And almost immediately, as soon as I had uttered this 'prayer' to God, the God I had stopped believing in as a teenager, my hands became completely steady—and yes, I mean instantly. It was like going from 100 mph to standing still, without any deceleration whatsoever! Then I looked up from the camp table I was sitting at, and saw the stars of the Milky Way and 'felt', for the first time in weeks, their beauty—and I thought to myself, why would I want to die? So I went into the tent and slept, the first good night's sleep I had had in a long time.

The next morning I woke up, refreshed, happy to be alive (the depression seeming like a bad dream, now over), and my vanity had returned: I would shave and shower. But as I walked towards a large building where the showers were, I felt 'something' come from behind me and into me, as it were, and before I got to that building I had begun shaking again, like a dried leaf blowing in the autumn wind, soon to fall to the dirt. I tried to shave but my hand shook so much I knew I would just cut myself.

And now I was desperate. I don't know why I was so naive the night before when weeks of suffering disappeared as soon as I sought a bit of help from the God I thought I had stopped believing in. It could have been the 'placebo effect', my mind did not want to die along with my body so its unconscious part shut down the depression—I am pretty sure this is how my shrink interpreted it when I told him about it. I might have agreed with him, except that it was not logical that my 'mind' would then return me and my body to that profound clinical depression, and make it even worse than before!

As we drove into Montpelier that morning I saw a bridge and knowing I had very little time left before I lost complete control, I told my friend to go for breakfast and I would join him after I walked some to 'calm down'. I walked to that bridge that spanned the spring-swollen Winooski River and hesitated! Not because of fear—I still saw death as extinction and so preferable to the living hell I didn't seem able to escape. Twice I walked to the ledge to jump but something pulled me back: I interpret it as the 'life force' that many writers have alluded to - whatever it is in us (and it is not fear) that wants to keep us alive. But I knew as I walked away the third time that if I did not do it then, I would not be able to later—so I turned and ran to the ledge, and flung myself over.

Because we don't forget the best or the worst in life, I remember like it was yesterday, and not 50 some years ago, how pleasant it was to fall through the air [I can understand why sky divers love their sport]. I don't remember hitting the water, but I do see myself going feet first through some rock-strewn rapids (I have a scar on my back from hitting one of those rocks, but thank God it was not my head!). I went unconscious briefly again it seems because my next memory is of finding myself swimming in the river, and as I saw the shore I thought to myself, why am I swimming, I want to die ... and I put my arms straight up and sank.

The next part is hard. Not hard to recall—if only! - but hard to relive, hard to accept I suppose. At some point I was conscious, not of having a body, just 'pure' consciousness. I have no doubt it's hard if not impossible to believe if you've never experienced it: Even in our dreams we have bodies. And I could see, but what I saw was an infinite darkness, far blacker than the darkest night. I was utterly alone and worse of all, in torment. I don't use that word lightly: it was beyond any imaginable pain and my consciousness was roiled by it. And again, I called out to God, not to end it but with a question: 'How long will it last?' To this day I have no idea why I asked that question.

When I regained 'this world' consciousness, I was on the bank of the river in a gurney being put into an ambulance—it lasted only seconds until I passed out again.

I spent four weeks on the psych ward and had a series of electroshock treatments, which appear to have done the trick in alleviating the depression. I began rebuilding my life, taking college courses for a new career and seeing a very good shrink for the next two years. He was a good man who helped me a great deal to explore my 'unconscious' side - talk therapy it's called today. But I'm sure he rationalized away the hellish experience of my un-bodied consciousness, my soul, as I was drowning in 12 feet of water.

I wish I could do so as well. Accepting the reality of hell can be terrifying, but I am a big fan of reason [which will surprise the secular minded]. And my reason tells me if things are not a matter of chance, but are directed by some Power or Mystery none of us can really comprehend, then 'God' could have as well left me there. The man who jumped into that river to save me was a Vietnam vet riding by on his Harley when he saw me jump. There were about 50 people on the river bank that day (so I was told) and nobody did anything, except for an ex-soldier who drove his bike to save my life.

I know our memories can play tricks on us, but usually it happens for the commonplace: getting a date or name mixed-up, thinking you did something when you hadn't. But from what I've read and have been told by others who've 'dipped' into the twilight zone', we don't forget trauma. And what could be more real than death, or the prospect of death? I wrote a little 'memoir' some 25 years after the event, and everything was as real then as it had been when I was 24—and it is all just as real—and yes, perplexing still, another 25 years later. But not just for me.

When I started taking some college classes for a new career, I met a young woman in one of the them. The mutual attraction we had was immediate and intense (a few months before when I was depressed I would have felt no attraction.) Soon we were living together, and while we had an inordinate amount of passion for each other, we never developed the friendship that I came to learn was the sine qua non for a long term relationship. if we had an argument we would just go make love to resolve it—and yes, we had a lot of arguments. Passion, especially very intense passion, really does need the ballast of friendship, to temper not its joy but its wildness ….

So one ordinary afternoon after our classes, we returned to our rented studio and made love, as we usually did in those heated days. No drugs, no drinking, we intoxicated each other enough. Suddenly I found myself outside my body, that is, my consciousness. I saw my then lean and youthful body between her legs (and 50 some years later I see it just as clearly) and though I could not see her own soul, I sensed it 'hovering' near mine—as she told me later she did mine. [I also remember clearly knowing it was my body but not feeling any 'attachment' to it—it seemed unimportant to my consciousness then, to my soul.] And then, as suddenly as we had left, we were back in our bodies.

To this day I see that shared experience as a great gift to both of us. I already had proof that I have a soul, but that awareness was gained in a very different circumstance. Over time several people have related their own 'out-of-body experiences' (OBEs) to me [people seem to relax with me when I share my own paranormal encounters and tell me things they say they don't readily share with others]. In my late 20's I was teaching ESL in Tokyo and one night having a beer at a bar with an Australian. He was a typical Aussie; friendly, down-to-earth, a surfer as far from 'mystical' as one might expect. He told me that one day he had been sunbathing on Bondi Beach near Sydney when suddenly he was about 50 feet up in the air looking down on himself and everyone else. He still seemed freaked out by it, emphasized that he wasn't drinking or on drugs—I smiled and told him, 'That was your soul'.

At the other end of life was a 91 year-old man I met at my health club a few years ago. I don't ask people if they believe in God - the question is too emotional, it seems, for both some believers and sceptics. Instead I ask if they think anything of themselves continues after death. He told me he didn't used to think so, until in his 40s one

Sunday when as usual his wife 'dragged' him to Mass with the family. Sitting bored as usual, he suddenly found himself, his consciousness, hovering beneath the nave of the large church, looking down on himself. his family and the entire congregation. As with myself and the Australian surfer, he soon found himself (his consciousness or soul) back in his body. He added as a postscript: 'After that I got in good with the priests.'

There are thousands of written accounts of NDEs and OBEs and other paranormal events, going back at last as far as Plato's telling of the near-death experience of the soldier of Ur after a great battle. I understand why many people are skeptical - I probably would still be an agnostic-materialist myself if I hadn't gone through what I did. The body-brain is such a complex organism that if you open a closet and something falls off a shelf, your hand will automatically reach out for it before your 'conscious' brain is even fully aware. And of course we've learned so much about medicine and science, but any good doctor will admit medicine is a much art as science [one question I like to ask MDs is if they know of patients who died who should have lived given their prognosis, as well as patients, whom their doctors had written off, surviving—and every one so far has said yes.]

And while I'm a great fan of science and its myriad benefits [I'm alive and walking because of it], it is important to remember that science is an impartial method, not a 'god'. Be it hi-def TV or your i-phone or thermonuclear weapons, science reflects our human interests and values, and is only concerned with the natural world, the universe we can measure. If there is a supernatural world permeating the natural one, science and scientists haven't a clue. We live in only three dimensions, four if you count time; the naked eye cannot see most of the spectrum of light, nor can the ear hear the full range of sound.

Because I live in a body in a material world, I have no idea how I could see without eyes or think without a brain, but I did—as apparently many others have over time. I know as I know I breathe that my 'self', my personal being, in some form or another has always existed and always will [though in what place may be the tricky part.] Can't prove any of it, but then I can't even prove I love my wife - but I'm beginning to realize only now as an old man, after being with her the better part of half a century, how much I do love her, though can I or anyone ever know how much of anything we are in this world of birth and death?

So I've come to suspect dying—the great universal human fear (and we seem to be the only species to fear it in the abstract) - may be akin to waking up shortly after a dream: You recall the dream, and how real it seemed whilst you were dreaming it, but now realize 'life' is reality, not the dream. And what about the tens of thousands of dreams you've had and don't even know you had them? Would it then be so surprising that if we are re-incarnated, as I suspect myself, we don't recall our past lives—save perhaps in bits and pieces. Like feeling an attachment to certain places, or taking an instant liking—or disliking—to someone you just met. Or perhaps the work you seek or the music or books you love?

The man was right: for the time being, we can only see through a glass darkly ….

THE LEAP

I was half-mad with despair,
Hopeless in love and life,
At the end of my rope--
so I chose to drown,
To cease all pain in
Sweet oblivion, to be
No more, to be gone….

And when I flung my
Young and strong body
Into that swollen river,
I thought that's what
Awaited me—nothing!
But oh I was so wrong,
For my agnostic mind
Could not foresee the
Awaiting vast blackness,
The pain beyond pain,
And the utter aloneness—
No other souls, none
But my bodiless mind
That had spurned God
And love as well, and
Now roiled in torment,
Until I called out to Him
And was released
From hell to return
To the world I had
So recently spurned.

Some will discount
This as the ravings

Of a young man
Breaking apart—
It's only fear, just
Imagined terrors,
Be brave they say,
Neither heaven nor
Hell awaits us, our
Only fate, extinction.

I might wish them
To be right, but
They are deluded—
As I once was, for
Now I know there
Is no way out, no
Escape from oneself,
From one's mind,
From one's soul….

ABOUT NOLO
Nolo only became a published poet as he neared his 8th decade, but has since had poems in published 35 literary magazines in the USA, UK, Canada, Romania, and India. In 2020, a trade publisher released a collection of his work titled, *The Enormity Of Existence*, and in 2021 another collection titled, *Of Earth and Earth*. Fifty years ago Nolo almost drowned in a Vermont river, and had a near-death experience which shattered his former faith in materialism; the idea that reality is only matter. He went from seeing life as meaningless, to knowing that the real problem was that there was so much meaning in everything - every action, every thought, every feeling. Being aware he has – is - a soul, an endless consciousness, may have helped him cope with teaching in the war zone of Cambodia, 1973-74 [leaving there about a year before the Killing Fields began]. He went on to teach ESL in Taiwan [where his wife is from] and Japan, before retunring back to the USA.
E: nolosegundo70@gmail.com

Poetry By Binod Dawadi

MY SISTER

My sister takes a lot of problems and tensions,
In her mind she can't handle her thoughts,
As well as she becomes out of control,
She doesn't eats foods,
She sits alone in the room,
As well as cry and shouts,
By thinking negative thoughts,
At first she thinks someone,
Is trying to kill her,
Someone is destroying her life,

She is living out from this world,
In her own world,
Where she is not happier,
She can't be normal like as us,
She can't live happily in her life,
She speaks rough words as well as,
Becomes a destructive,
She breaks the glasses of houses or neighbours,
She breaks the things and makes them,
In the pieces she gives troubles to,

The family and friends,
We don't know what is happening,
We know that she is not mentally fit,
She have some problems,
One day she took a knife and tried,
To kill herself at 12:00pm at night,
When she do such activities she use,
To shout and cry, she shout and cry,
I listen to her and stop her,
I look at her at whole night,

At last we don't have any solutions,
To this problems our one neighbour,
Told that she is suffering from depression,
She should be taken to the hospital,
Our sister had also such problems,
We took her to the hospital,
Doctors check and give the patient medicines,

From which they can sleep and this problems can be solved,
We did the same we took her to hospital,
Doctor check her and give her medicines,

She stay for hospital for some months,
After sometimes she sleeps in night nicely,
As well as this problem is solved,
She should take medicine in her entire life,
If she will stops the medicine,
This disease depression will be seen,
We know that this is a dangerous disease,
If it is not cared patient can be mad and,
Takes life patient can do anything,
Can try to harm self, things or people in this disease.

ABOUT THE POEM
"This is the real experience of my sister. I want to tell and share my thoughts to the world through this poem. How is depression caused? How it can affect our life? How suicide and abnormal behaviour is seen by others, and how we can treat this disease and control suicide? Her problems is not only her problems, but the problems of the world. My sister is my life. I love her so much, but I must always take care of her, and look to see if she has any abnormal behaviours and activities; for example she used to move her head around like ghosts move, cut up her clothes, destroy things in house, and cries and and shouts when she is out of control, which causes me a great deal of stress and tension in my life. And so I think about her, and observe her, and write all these things on paper in the form of stories and poetry. It helps to give me some motivation and inspiration, and at this time, writing is often my only friend."

ABOUT BINOD
Binod is from Kathmandu, Nepal. He has completed his Master's Degree from Tribhuvan University in Major English. He likes to read and write, and has created many poems and stories. His hobbies are also singing, watching movies, travelling and gardening. He is a creative person, who is always helping the poor, and believes from writing and art, it is possible to change people's knowledge, views and perspectives towards many things, including mental illness.
E: vinoddawadi9@gmail.com

Poetry by Donna McCabe

BREAKDOWN

I am still standing
After things that I have seen
Feeling better now
Than I have ever been.
I have searched my soul
Broke free of my past
Discovering myself
At long last.
Shed fears and anxieties
That for so long kept me down
Now swimming on the current
On which I almost drowned.
So here I stand
Tall and proud
Looking forward to a new tomorrow
I have brushed off all doubts and fears
And have no more sorrows

SURVIVOR

Having to live on
Just living life
Musing on the what could have been
An endless turmoil without you
Missing that well loved voice
Misery squeezes at this heart
Always lonely
In spite of others
As I am left
To this adventure on my own
Having loved and lost
And lived on.

TRUTH

A crushing blow
The flare of anger
The truth not seeming to be believed

The hurt and pain
It raises again
After a long and slumbered sleep
A heart that has yearned a kiss or a hug
Or a simple "I love you"
There's a barrier up
And it won't descend
For reasons just left alone
The hurt inside is like furnace blazing
The past and present collide
Is there shame or proudness
Who can tell
Who wants to really know
Could we handle it if we knew?

IN NEED OF LOVE

Suffering in silence
Dying inside
Suppressed by doom and gloom
Wanting to be happy
To smile,to laugh
To much distance
From here to there
Feeling alone
With no one to hold
Tears of a lonely heart fall
In need of love
Of a sunny glade
Full of hope and joy
Not wanting to crash and burn.

EXHAUSTED

So sick of life
Getting dealt a crappy hand
Dreams blown out the window
Nothing going to plan
All glum and gloomy
Behind this fake smile
A failure,a loser
A brain on the blink
Thoughts so dark

I try not to think
Useless for anything
What can I offer
No job would employ
No contribution to the coffer
Alone with dark ideas
Racking my brain
I cry and I sob
Feel like I'm going insane
Am I just having a down day
Or is it something more
That old friend depression
Knocking on my door???

DARK REFLECTIONS

I see myself
But I'm not really here
My mind is far away elsewhere
Dreaming of other things
Dark sombre things
I don't think anyone would understand
These dark thoughts are a reflection
Of the smile I paint on every day
Pretending everything's just fine and dandy
When really it's just dark and dysfunctional.

ABOUT THE POEMS
"The poems were written as a way of dealing with difficult and dark periods of my life, some of which I'm still dealing with to this day. I lost my dad to suicide at 15, and still had many other difficult hurdles to content with, as well as trying to process what he'd done too. It still has major impacts to this very day, as well as managing my own health issues of epilepsy and mental health. I do believe personally that the therapy of writing has brought me much joy and healing over the years, and helped soothe a lot of the pain."

ABOUT DONNA
Based in the picturesque valleys of the Rhondda, South Wales, Donna is an established poet with over 20 years experience whose vast variety of work has gained her multiple accolades within her field of literature. She has been published in many magazines, anthologies and journals including: T*he Writers and Readers' Magazine, Our Poetry Archive, Raven Cage Zine, Words in Motion, Movement Our*

Bodies In Action, Jewels in the Queens Crown: The Best Of The Best, The Sacred Feminine Volume II, Quintessence: Coming of Age, Nobody Left Behind, Hidden In Childhood, Our Seasons of Syllables, and *Our Changing Earth.* Her intricate wordplay displayed in her work has been personified by her past and concurrent experiences, which include her hardships, trials and tribulations. All of which she has been accompanied by her loving husband of 25 years, and their three children. Her lifetime admiration of reading and writing, and love of art has recently steered her into a adventurous new direction of collaborations with an up and coming Canadian artist Ala Ilescu whose idiosyncratic mind and artistic works compliment the vivid images Donna's narrative works paint. These collaborations have resulted in a beautiful book of poetry and artwork entitled *Explosion Of Love*. Donna's creativity has also taken her onto other platforms in recent times, Using Instagram to reach out and display her love of writing, artwork and love of the natural world to a wider audience.
FB:@ Poemsbydonnamccabe
Instagram: @donnamccabe_

Poetry by Frances Gaudiano

MY SILVER FRIEND

My friend is sharp, shiny and cool.
So sharp that her touch
Leaves behind bubbles of blood.
I stare fascinated at her trail,
A red kiss,
A gift.

She cuts the cord to the noisy world.
I can breathe, slow and deep,
Admiring her steps along my arm, dripping.
She has removed the disease
And I sit peaceful, complete as a stone.

Thanking my silver friend,
I wrap her in foil and put her away,
Safe.
Until the next time I need her.

FREQUENT FLYER

Furtively I disembark,
Carry -on my sole companion.
No welcome hug on arrival.
The drawers in this new house are empty.

Each night, in search of sleep,
I fill the laundry with worn out costumes.
Till naked, I see the lump.
Malignant, it leers while eating me.
Parasites can travel too.
Running rearranges the location,
But never stills their gluttony.

Today, I am a surgeon,
Knife poised; I dissect myself.
Excise the reeking tumour,
Years lost and spoiled
Waiting for the courage.

My flesh gapes,
Weak fingers stutter through the sutures.
Repaired, I stand still,
For the first time ever.

ICONOCLAST

I was a candle that burned too brightly.
I was a bird that flew too high.
The world snared and held me tightly,
Snuffed my flame and made me cry.
I was a voice that sang out loud.
I was a night that dreamed too long.
Critics damned me, called me proud,
Acid words stilled my song.
I was a child with games immense.
I was a heart that leapt too far.
Distrust, betrayal became my fence,
Mischief wins no golden stars.
Careful actors learn their lines,
Study movement, parading grace.
The proper words were never mine,
The wrong expression dressed my face.
I lost instructions right away,
And stumbled on the untrod path.
Warm homes chase off the unkept stray,
Animal control collects the trash.

ABOUT THE POEMS
"I have always felt cutting was a release, a method of preventing something worse happening. I am not proud to say I have been cutting for the past forty years, however, I am proud to say that I have survived. You have to do what you have to do to make it to the next day."

ABOUT FRANCES
Frances lives in Cornwall, England, and is a veterinary nurse and practising druid. Her novel, *The Listener,* was published last year, and two other projects are in the editing stages. She has had poetry published in a variety of journals and hopes to produce a chapbook soon.

Poetry by Mia Amore Del Bando

BACK TO DUST

My family sits in the corner
Wondering why would I ever want to visit God
With a gently tied rope
Or a misfire of a gun

God's been missing my prayers
And dodging the voicemails
Miscommunication that no church can conveniently tie
As if He was on speed dial, a starred favorite

I wanted to ask
If there was a plan
And if we were a mistake
That simply got of hand

I sit under fat clouds
Wipe the tears
Pour myself a drink
And breed a new hope for tomorrow

From to dust
Back to dust
My family sits in a corner
Wondering why I left
Devastated I can never visit again

AFTER THE PARTY

Today the sun is pretending to be the moon
Everything is in slow motion
Must have left my brain at home
With all the responsibilities
Burning the list with a match

Last night I decided to leave
Dive into the party
Label me a forever M.I.A.
Maybe I can live down there
Where no one knows my name

Strangers kissing me to forget their exes
Memory gifts me with fragments

Today is odd
As the wind plays with my hair
Outside cool like glass against my skin
Whispering
"What happened?"
Adding another missing puzzle piece
Without a picture reference

All I remember is that I missed you
You left me in a dream
Where I called and you picked up
Before I could say I love you
I turned into dust

ABOUT THE POEMS
"These poems reflect on the cruel thought process of self-harm and suicide. I wrote these to resist any temptation. At times, I feel small, and writing helps me create a better relationship with myself, and a higher power in able to pull myself out of negative thinking. Negative and suicidal thoughts are addictive, and you have to develop the self-awareness to spot it early. Writing is my outlet, and my savior."

ABOUT MIA
Mia was born and raised in Long Beach, California, and is a Los Angeles based flight attendant. She has been featured in *The Art of Everyone, You Might Need To Hear This, Flora Fiction, Inlandia*, and others. Her work has also been published in-print by Wingless Dreamer and Poets Choice.
E: miadelbando@gmail.com
Instagram: @miaamoure

Poetry by Jane H. Fitzgerald

CALLING IT QUITS

Ethel was ninety-five
When she decided
It was time to get out
She was just tired of it all
She had had it
Not one of her generation left
Family buried in faraway places
Including one of her beloved sons
Everyone was young and energetic
Everything was new and challenging
She didn't belong anymore
Dehumanizing electronics ruled
Language and actions on TV
Were rude and perplexing
Did she really share the planet
With these strange strangers
She had come from an old
More gentile world
The way people interacted
Now lacked civility
No one held the door for her
Or gave up their seat on the bus
She felt alone, isolated
It was such an effort to continue
To get up, get dressed, get going
Face the world
Call the plumber
Deal with the garden
Go to the grocery store
What used to be simple pleasures
Were now unpleasant chores
So even though she believed in God
(She had been a minister's wife)
She had had it
What was the point
Why should she keep on struggling
When everyday just got harder
More physical pain, deeper mental alienation
So at ninety- five, tired and worn out
And basically sick of it all

Ethel called it quits

ABOUT THE POEM
"This poem is about my grandfather's sister who lived to be well into her nineties. It explains her feelings about outliving her contemporaries, and even her child."

ABOUT JANE
Jane lives in Florida, USA, and is a retired history teacher who writes poetry with clarity, compassion and insight. Jane has been writing for over thirty years since she studied poetry with David Ignatow at Columbia University, where she earned a MA Degree. She has written four books including, *Notes From the Undaunted*. Her poetry has been featured in *The Poet, Your Daily Poem, Isele Magazine, Open Door Magazine, Dreamers Creative Writing, Sad Girls Club, Quillkeepers Press*, and more. She hopes that others will find comfort and a sense of togetherness through her poetry. She embraces the young, old, all nationalities and creeds. Jane loves peace and promotes harmony through her work.
E: jane.fitzgerald2@gmail.com

Poetry by George Colkitto

EMPTY THOUGHTS FROM A FULL MIND

Take all the tablets
Drink all the wine
At least when you die
You'll be smiling

Take out the car
Drive into the sea
or pick a lamp-post
pick a tree
Hit it at speed and bang
you are gone
What if you failed
and you lived on?

Take all the tablets
Drink all the wine
At least when you die
You'll be smiling

Jump from on high
Jump into the sea
But what of the moment
Braced for the landing
What of the panic
finding you're drowning

Take all the tablets
Drink all the wine
At least when you die
You'll be smiling

ABOUT THE POEM
"I am a great believer in the power of writing to help with the problems everyone faces. Writing these poems helped me in what were very dark times. Although I did once sit with all my warfarin tablets on the table and knew if I took them that would be it, I doubt I was ever really serious about suicide, but I came close on a few occasions,, so it easy - with hindsight - to believe I couldn't do it."

ABOUT GEORGE

George is an ex- Inspector of Taxes, Chartered Account, and bookshop owner. He writes both poetry and prose, and has had short stories and poetry published in magazines and anthologies including *Ink Sweat and Tears, Envo*i and *Poetry Scotland*. Successful in a number of competitions, his commissioned poems are on permanent display in Linwood Johnstone, and Erskine Health Centres. He lives in Scotland and is on the Scottish Book Trust Live Literature Directory, and has facilitated workshops for NHS Renfrewshire Network Services, Lochwinnoch Arts Festival and Cinnamon Press.

W: www.gwcolkitto.co.uk.

FB: @George Colkitto Writer

Poetry by Duane Anderson

REST IN PEACE

Why was it I liked sleeping during the day,
closing my eyes as I sat in my chair
shortly after waking up in the morning,
taking naps in the afternoon,
falling asleep while watching television
when all I really want to do
is sleep soundly at night?

The time may have final come for me
to adjust my sleep patterns to full time,
pulling the covers over me,
one consisting of a grass blanket
over a layer of dirt,
keeping me warm
in my new eternal bed.

LIFE SENTENCE

I was given a life sentence,
being born into this world,
life without parole.

One where I did not have total control,
and elements I could not change
no matter how hard I tried.

I learned about love,
I learned about hate,
I've learned about truth and justice.

Do what you want to do to me.
I can only do so much.
Your time will come, and mine is here.

It has been good knowing you.
I've done my time on earth,
as I say goodbye, so long.

A STEP BACK

Correct me if I am wrong?
No, don't correct me,
I do not wish to know.
I have been told what to do,
to say, my entire life.
If I'm right, that's okay.
If I'm wrong, that's okay too.
No more of life's lessons for me,
I'm tired of following the crowd.
Right or wrong, it no longer matters,
I'm going on my own,
wherever that may take me.
Maybe one day, I will see you again.

ABOUT DUANE
After graduating from Augustana College, South Dakota, USA, and working at Union Pacific Railroad for 37 years, Duane retired in 2013 and started writing poetry again - after too long of an absence. He has had poems published in *Poetry Quarterly, Fine Lines, Cholla Needles, Tipton Poetry Journal, Adelaide Literary Magazine, Aura Literary Arts Magazine*, and several other publications. He is the author of *Yes, I Must Admit We Are Neighbors* (Cyberwit.net 2021), *On the Corner of Walk and Don't Walk*, (Pacific Poetry Press 2021), and *The Blood Drives: One Pint Down* (Cyberwit.net 2022). His latest poetry book is *Conquer the Mountains* (Cyberwit.net 2022).
E: danderson7575@cox.net
FB: @duane.anderson.710667

Timothy Paul Brown's story

The first symptom I can look back on and say that I had was dissociation. It started when I would walk to school with my brothers. As we were walking, I would lose consciousness, and would come back to consciousness by bumping into a telephone pole. I had no recollection of what happened. My brothers would laugh at me. I was only 8 years-old. This was back in 1972. There wasn't much known about dissociation at that time, so my family didn't know what to do or think about it.

I come from a very dysfunctional background. My father was very physically abusive, and my brother sexually abused me up until the age of eight ... that was around the same time that I started dissociating. I started experimenting with cigarettes around that time as well, and running away from home. All my acting out and getting into trouble started around the same time of being sexually abused. I lost a lot of my memory, and have a distorted understanding about what sexuality is. I've felt tremendous guilt and shame over the years about my sexual experiences; and still feel that guilt and shame in the form of flashbacks. I have developed PTSD from my childhood years, as well as a result of being abused physically and mentally within the mental health system.

I started using drugs at the age of 11. I've been told that my drug use exacerbated my mental illness. I tried drugs like marijuana, cocaine, cigarettes, alcohol, mescaline and angel dust. I was never a heavy drug user, it was what would happen to me as a result of using: I would hear voices. I would see things. I thought I was God. I would have rituals and superstitions. I became super paranoid. And eventually I became very depressed. I was diagnosed with a paranoid schizophrenic disorder, which later became a schizoaffective disorder. I used drugs sporadically over the years. Every time I had the same result; the paranoia, the hallucinations, the delusions, the grandiosity, the obsession compulsion, and the depression. I tried going to Narcotics Anonymous and Alcoholics Anonymous meetings. After years of going there I realized that I wasn't an alcoholic or drug addict at all. I'm a mentally ill person whose life was in danger every time I decided to use. I was there with hard-core drug addicts. These people used more drugs in one month than I did in my whole life! The good thing that came out of it is that I stopped the destructive behaviour. I haven't had a drop of alcohol and haven't used a substance since December of 1996. I even quit smoking cigarettes in June of 2005. I don't even use caffeine. I now live a very clean life.

The first time I started hearing voices was at the age of 17. I would hear voices coming from miles away. They would talk to me, and they would talk to each other. They would say things like they are going to kill and rape me. I spent a lot of my life in the shelter system. I first experienced homelessness at the age of 18. When I was on the street, I took a hallucinogen called mescaline. That was my introduction into the mental health system; I started seeing things which seemed so real to me. I started seeing the face of what appeared to be a devil on the face of the person that gave me the mescaline pill. I started hearing this crazy voice. His pupils became pinpoint. His ears sharpened and his teeth grew fangs.

After that happened, I was going around town accusing people of being possessed. The police picked me up and brought me to jail. When they realized I was sick, they transferred me to a forensic unit at the jail. Then they sent me to Rockland State Psychiatric Center in Rockland County, New York. This was back in 1983. They put me on Thorazine. My tongue started swelling and my eyes rolled back into my head. Until they gave me Cogentin for the side effects. This was only one of many traumatic experiences in my life. This was my entrance into the world as a young man. Most of us usually go to college, have a girlfriend, get their first car, maybe even get an apartment. This was not the case for me. No one - man or woman - should experience these things at such a young age! I have been in and out of hospitals from the age of 18 to the age of 52. I have had over 30 hospitalizations. On my second hospitalization, I experienced the most terrible hallucinations. I was seeing and hearing things that weren't there. It was so real to me that I have remnants of those memories in my head even today. And in my mind, they are still real sometimes. I am able to rationalize and reality check though. But the impact is still there. It's like a computer program running in the background. The voices were so loud and the visual was as clear as what the average person sees every day. As a result of my hallucinations, I tried to kill myself every chance I could get; I was consistently trying to hang myself but always got caught and stopped. I wanted to die so badly. I had tried killing myself numerous times in my life. One time I swallowed rat poison. A few times I tried to overdose on my pills. Once I tied my shirt around my neck and tied it to a tree and jumped. My shirt snapped ... and here I am to tell the story! This was in 1993. That was the last time I have ever tried to hurt myself. I have been very suicidal since then but have never attempted suicide again. I realize that I must be here for a reason. I promised myself no matter how bad things get, suicide is not a solution.

Most of my story I have blocked out to protect my mind. I have lost time for weeks at a time. There are parts of my life that I will never get back because of it. I struggle with that a lot. However, as the years go by, I am getting glimpses and pieces of my past.

I don't believe in sugar coating the truth. I believe it is my responsibility to tell the truth as I see it. I cannot hold back. I believe that I write about things that we all have experienced. I write about things that we all have thought about. I have been praised for giving people something to identify with. As well as being given courage to deal with everyday life. I have given many of us reason to love ourselves through my poetry. I have helped put people on a path of healing through my poetry. Thus, healing is poetic!

I started having the worst panic attacks. I still have them today. There is one place I have not gone back to in over 30 years because of a terrible panic attack I had. I cannot be in closed places with a lot of people. There must be a way for me to leave and quickly or I will have a meltdown. I have embarrassed myself as a result of melting down in front of people. They all called me crazy. I couldn't take buses or trains for years because of it. Airports and subways are a nightmare for me. It took years of therapy and personal effort for me to overcome my panic attacks. I still have my issues with it today. At this point I can ride the buses and trains. I can go to NYC. I belong to a gym that I frequent. I'm not so afraid of people. My social skills have improved tremendously.

My progress started in 1984 when I was put on the drug Prolixin. That was when I started a medication regiment. I tried to get off the medications in 1985 and 1998. I thought I was cured. I think most of us have experienced that. But I have been taking my medications without fail since 1998. I truly learned my lesson. I now know the importance of taking medications. I started therapy with a therapist by the name of Dr Straytner. He was the first male that I bonded with since the time I came into the mental health system.

I have had numerous therapists since then. They all played a different role in my life. The most important and pivotal point in my therapy came with my present therapist Linda A. We have developed an unbreakable bond over the last five years. It is a partnership. We talk about everything. I teach her, and she teaches me. Our relationship is very reciprocal. I've helped her to look at psychotherapy in new ways. She knows how to treat me naturally at this point. I have had doctors and therapists literally call me crazy because of the way I think. I think it threatens their intelligence. Linda has never done that. She has been a godsend. I have never covered and uncovered more in all the years I have been in therapy.

However, I still have a lot of grievances towards some of the treatment I have received over the years. I find that we all have grievances in the system. A great majority of us are afraid to express them for fear of being put away or given more medication as a result. Some of us don't know how to express our grievances. We just respond to whatever treatment we receive. A great majority of us are afraid to be who we are for those same reasons. We feel we must fit in just to be right with the world. We feel isolated sometimes. A lot of us feel controlled. A lot of us don't realize that we are actually a different kind of people. We think differently. We feel differently. We perceive differently. We process information differently. We act differently. We will never be whole or on a path to recovery until we recognize and accept that about ourselves. That is the major reason why I write.

My journey with poetry when I started writing at the age of ten. My very first poem was entitled *Fats*. It was about an overweight child whom kids would beat up and tease because he was overweight. It is what they would call bullying and fat shaming today. I was able to see that in 1974 as a 10 year-old kid. I have always been told that I have a lot of insight and vision. I carry this through my poetry. I didn't start writing on a regular basis until about the age of 21. I remember I was hospitalized. I met a young poet whose poetry really took me aback. I was totally amazed by his style. He would make four sentences that all rhymed and then go onto another four sentences. He would make maybe 16 bars. The content of his poetry amazed me. This young gentleman took my poetry on a different path. I wrote a lot of poems while I was there. My poems were thrown in the garbage because they weren't considered practical to my mom. In any case my love for poetry remained. The oldest poem that I have in existence was written in 1988. I actually have the original. 1997 is when I really started writing. I was working the graveyard shift at a gas station. I would write in-between customers. I had a lot of time to write. At the time my greatest influence was a rapper by the name of Tupac Shakur. His mental anguish and conflict between good and evil really did it for me. Then in 1998 there was a rapper by the name of DMX that exploded on the scene whose work really intrigued and inspired me. His conflict between God and his street life was amazing to me. In 2002 I bought a CD from a friend of mine entitled *My own prison*. It was from a band by the name of *Creed*. When I heard the title song *My own prison*, it changed the way I write. I arrived! It was the conflict I felt that inspired me. I felt the pain. I felt the confusion. I felt the religiosity in their work. There was a myriad of emotions and ideas that came from their lyrics. I am a lyricist, so the lyrics from songs are the most impactful on my style of writing. The music helped too. I took the intensity and the passion that I felt and made it my own. I used my own subject matter. I used my own thoughts, ideas, processes, and perceptions and put it in poetic form.

There is a psychosocial club here in Westchester County by the name of HOPE HOUSE. I would go there at least three times a week. I would sit at their computers and start writing. I found myself writing a poem a day. I would listen to music as I wrote. The energy from the music and the energy from the room, along with my thoughts, is what made for the quality of my work. I would just create. I am in my zone when I am writing. It is my high. It takes me to places I never imagined. People would tell me how talented I was. To me it was survival. I never thought I could do something with my work. I had a life changing operation back in 2021. After I started to recover, I got the idea to publish my work. I put all my work together and from there I published my first book *Poetic Madman*. Shortly after that I published my second book *Twisted Rage*. Thirdly I published *A Man Divided*. And lastly *Genius or Lunatic*. I made a lot of mistakes throughout the whole process. It was a lot of trial and error. But I finally got it done. I created a website *Healing is Poetic* during that time. It gives people an understanding of what it is like to have a mental illness. It gives practitioners, loved ones, consumers, anyone interested in knowing more about us, insight. It goes deep into what we think about. What we've been through and what we need as a people. Which is mainly love and compassion.

I believe poetry is a form of expression that brings us as a people together. Poetry can be a vehicle towards self-healing. I believe it empowers us in a world that can be unforgiving.

I used to live in a perceived threatening world. Some of it real and some of it not. None of it fabricated. What people don't realize is that none of this is made up. It doesn't mean that what we perceive is real. It just means that it is not made up. What we go through are real experiences just by the fact that we experience it. Everyone should be able to trust their own perceptions. It is one of the most basic human needs. The ability to trust one's perceptions. To us what we go through is absolutely real. It seems that we as a people are the only ones taught that we can't trust our own perceptions. And sometimes we are persecuted when we do. Sadly, sometimes by the people who care for us. I'm so grateful that it is only an emergency when we are seen as suicidal or homicidal. It means that we can think and feel however we choose as long as we are not a threat to ourselves or others. That is so liberating. I have been waiting for that all my life. I come from a time when anyone can have you committed if you were acting a bit off. I come from a time when anyone could call one of your practitioners and get information about you. There was no protection for the mentally ill. There was no HIPPA law. This made me gun-shy about expressing my thoughts and feelings. Today I feel freer. That's how I was able to fearlessly create my website. That's how I am able to unapologetically express who I am.

I am in my zone when I am writing. It is my high. It takes me to places I never imagined. Self-expression, to me, is vital to our recovery. In my experience poetry has given me great courage. I think it can do the same for all poets with mental disabilities. It is a form of therapy. I have been in poetry classes at my psychosocial club HOPE HOUSE. I've seen members from HOPE HOUSE come alive when writing poems. Even those with no experience at all benefit from writing. I've seen it first-hand. I saw faces light up when the instructor would come. It was the highlight of the week for many of us. I know from my own experience that poetry gives self-esteem, self-worth, and true pride to persons like myself. I believe it gives us purpose and meaning.

Poetry is my saving grace. I will always say that. It is the most powerful tool of self-expression for me. I love poetry! And poetry loves me!

A DOSE OF MEDICINE AWAY

Psychosis is just a dose of medicine away
Or lack thereof should I say
I do not want it; I am sick of it you see
It takes away the very vital parts of me
Like my thought patterns and its fluidity
My philosophies and religiosity
My love and my plausibility
My desires to fulfil my sexual needs
Destroys every hope and every dream
Makes my temperament turn from pleasant to mean

Here are the alternatives to my non-compliance
I will go from lucidity to not making sense
I will become fearful without reason
I will obsess over if I am a Christian or heathen
I will confuse love and abuse
Maybe I'll hang from a noose
Maybe I'll destroy any sense of affection
Rebel from any kind of correction
Daring sensibility to come my direction
Never caring about the negative attention
Descending emotionally instead of ascending
Falling into the abyss and hellish dimensions

Is this what I want to be sick in the head?
To be demented and spiritually dead
To have no control over my faculties
To become victim to all of the fallacies
Like schizoid people are violent and cannot be trusted

Like we will never be stable or mentally adjusted
Like we are a cancer with no answers at all
Like if we accept them, it will be our downfall
Don't let them near weapons especially guns
Their irrationality is second to none
They are possessed and need to be exorcised
The children they create will grow up despised

The alternative is black and white with no shades of gray
In my experience I can truthfully say
The sanity I desire is just a dose of medicine away
It determines if I'll be okay

WHERE WERE YOU?

Daddy, have I brought you to anger?
Is my mother in danger?
I witnessed terror as you whipped my brother
And I begged for you to stop strangling my mother
You gave us pain and agony and at what cost
Just to confess your sins at the foot of the cross
I am a child of God whose spirit has grown cold
You see I died in my heart a long time ago
And I never asked for all this abuse in my life
I never asked to see my daddy batter his wife
Oh, you hid it well so that I could not see
Well, I saw you at four, but you didn't see me
Come to think of it that was my first memory
Why did you have to take that from me?
My heart wanted to find you
The man deep inside you
In hopes that I could reach your mind
And heal the sickness that hides you
And try to forgive you
Where were you?
I ask you daddy did I do something wrong?
Was it my fault you and mommy did not get along?
I ask you again daddy did I do something wrong?
Was it my fault that you did not come home?
Home in my heart where my soul needed you
In my spirit and mind that bled for you
But you never showed up
And God knows it hurt so much
Now I love an image that was never there

Always dreaming that you would somehow appear
Show up in my life and wipe my tears
And to tell me that you will always be here
You said in life the good always outweighs the bad
So, you tell me where was the good in the relationship we had?
And it can never be reconciled because you are gone
And I can't help but think it was something that I did wrong
My mind grows weary my heart becomes heavy
And my only recourse is sad
But I must reject your memory
Because it hurts so much dad
Where were you?

I ENJOY MY DELUSIONS

I live in a world where my delusions reign
Reality for me could never be the same
Euphoria and fear are always there
Prayers to the almighty dissipates in the air
Never-ending, mind-bending thoughts
It's like hanging from a cliff then falling off
Spiraling down into the abyss
Strange understandings come from my lips
I do not think as other people do
Can my paranoid delusions be based on truth?
Truth is far from my range of understanding
Answers to my questions is all I'm demanding
It seems like everything I think is wrong
I'm trying to find a place where I belong
I lose out on life, and I'm told this is love
Never knowing what I'm really made of
Discouraged to follow any form of mindset
I'm taught to forget
I'm a ward of the state considered a bastard
Doubting myself is all that I've mastered

Ridiculed for my illegible chatter
To them my humiliation doesn't even matter
They sedate me with this mind-bending substance
Then they threaten me to give up my madness
They treat me like I'm not even a person
Then they give me a needle when I start cursing
They do this considered for my safety
Basically, saying that everything about me is crazy

The treatment they give me in my weakened state
Has sealed my doom and my lifelong fate
Encouraged never to procreate
Never to support each other or try to relate
All because they fear our minds
Forever trying to keep us blind
Afraid to let society get near us
Keep us under wraps so nobody hears us
So, you see world I live in my delusions
They protect me from society
They put a barrier between you and me
Can't you see this is a world made just for me
Don't take it away!!!

MISTREATMENT

I cannot afford to be locked on this ward
With inhumane treatment as my reward
I hear voices telling me the food is poisoned
My mind is sensitive to outside noises
I am not an experiment so don't test my temperament
Let me feel what I feel so I won't feel resentment
You call me non-compliant
all I did was deny this medication and its science
I rely on you for my sanity
so please show me some humanity
You people give me needles
when in my mind I think they are lethal
I'm scared I fear that I will be killed
by your methods and pills
Yet and still, you give me medicine against my will
I know I'm unusual
but not everything is corrected by pharmaceuticals
Why do you rush me?
take me down, break me and crush me
I developed real fears of you through the years
I question if any one of you cares
Therapy is telling me that everything is wrong with me
meanwhile I long to be
rid of this pain
I truly want to sustain
but something is bugging me inside of my brain
These beds are so cold
It's like inside my soul

the food doesn't feed it, it's filthy with mold
the men and women are distanced and separate
and affection is discouraged to our discredit
You see we need love and touch just like everyone else
So just maybe we can learn to love ourselves

DON'T TELL ME

Don't tell me I'm crazy those are hurtful words
When you say I'm a misfit those words really hurt
Don't tell me what I hear isn't real
Don't tell me it's wrong to feel what I feel
Don't tell me I'm paranoid when I think you will hurt me
I have a doctor and therapist who will assess and observe me
Don't call me grandiose if I think I am famous
Or if I think I am God don't call me shameless
Don't call me delusional when I think my mind is being read
Don't think I'll commit suicide just because I wished I was dead
Don't say I'm hallucinating when I see things that aren't there
Don't use me or abuse me because of my fears
If you say that you love me, you will accept me for me
And support all that I desire as well as my dreams
If you say that you love me then please don't judge me
Treat me like everyone else if you really do love me
You are my mother, my lover, my father, my best friend
See
You are the people who should fight and defend me
I don't need another doctor who treats me
I need a human being who will love and complete me
Don't tell me I'm too emotional when I scream, and I cry
But tell me you are there for me
And that you'll always be by my side

ABOUT TIM
Timothy comes from a very dysfunctional and abusive background; his father was physically abusive to his mom, his siblings and himself, and he was sexually abused by his brother up until the age of eight. Diagnosed with schizophrenia, which later became a schizoaffective disorder, and in and out of psychiatric hospitals for most of his life, poetry has been his saving grace, and one of the most powerful tools of discovery and self-expression.
E: timbrownspoetry@gmail.com
W: www.healingispoetic.com

Poetry by Pam Ski

SING A SONG

Give a cheer for mischief,
Pockets bulging with fun,
Off on mad adventures, our
darling, dare-do-well son.

Thrum the drums of suspense,
Buckets brimming with Thrills,
Carnival of capers,
Vivid ... Devil-may-kill.

Rap those risky habits,
Rockets of drugs and booze,
Staking his peace of mind,
No sense of win or lose.

Chant the chimes of crazy,
Baskets of clutching straws,
Reeling merry go round
Of locked revolving doors.

Sing a song of painless,
Pockets empty. Disbelief.
Jumped ship at twenty-seven,
Dumped all his Joie de vivre.

Pluck the soul with sorrow,
A stitch of strange relief,
Patchwork of spilled ashes,
The odds and sods of grief.

Strum the strings of guilty,
Seams stretched taut with doubt,
Stuff done, stuff not done, to
Turn torment inside out.

Sing a song of painful
Pockets ripped and torn
A young man's life in
tatters, a family left to mourn

Look back at old photos,
Catch a glimpse of his smile,
Cling onto him for a second
Its been such a long while.

Flick through old school-stories...
stick-men dance on the page,
Faded pencil scribbling...such
humour, such insight...such rage

Sing a song of longing,
Pockets wrung out with regret,
Seasons sprint right past me
I face backwards in my head.

ABOUT THE POEM
"I wrote this poem after my son took his own life while suffering with drug-induced schizophrenia. I was sat in the car and 'Suicide is Painless' by the Manic Street Preachers came on the radio. A random thought came into my head: 'sing a song of suicide, they might as well sing a song of sixpence'. That thought led to the poem. These days I write a lot of different types of poems, but it's the focus needed to write that helps me to manage my stress."

AS I WAITED

Felt your presence,
swaddled in
your safe 'n
soundness.

Felt your flutter,
Dreamt your future:
Weighted by
your feather
fingers.

Jump of panic!

Burning ice of
thumping fear,

Felt my heart
pumping in

my ear.

Scared to mention,

Dared to question...

Soothing words of
wishful thinking...

Dragged along by
life and living,

Drifting, sinking,
drifting.

ABOUT PAM
"I am not on meds. I am OK as long as I keep off caffeine and alcohol; they make me instantly wired or over-jolly, respectively; my mind flaps about in my head looking to become unhinged ... I walk my own bumpy path of highs, lows, anxiety, depression, but they're bumps not hills or ruddy great mountains. Can still trip in a pothole though ... I watch myself."

Poetry by Jacquelyn Alexander

I'M NOT SELFISH

My mom says suicide is selfish.
I wonder if she thinks
you get to attend
your own funeral—

As if God lets you hover
above your casket
like a solemn grey cloud
and tally every tear.

Like you might linger
to see if the sanctuary is
shoulder to shoulder,
littered with sodden tissues.

Or if it's barren
aside from empty pews
and the echoes
of a few shuffling feet—

I wonder if she said that
because she knows
I'm afraid my funeral
will only be
reverberations
of clacking heels,
and not sniffles
and snot-bubbles that
interrupt
songs and speeches—

I wonder if
that's why I decided
to stay.

ABOUT THE POEM
"'I'm Not Selfish' was very therapeutic to write. My mom has told me on more than one occasion that suicide is selfish, and I've always been upset by that comment, because mental illness is not a choice. A little over a year ago, I was diagnosed with Bipolar II disorder, and

since then I've been recognizing times in my life that were ridiculously difficult because I was unmedicated and dealing with this illness. I can think of many times where I had suicidal thoughts that I denied because my mom told me how selfish it is, and I didn't want to die a selfish death or cause her any harm. I didn't want to be remembered as a selfish person. In the poem wanted to depict two types of funerals: one that is full, and on that is mostly empty. Because of what my mom said, I have always feared a funeral that is empty. I think there are a lot of people who can relate to this fear so that's why I wanted to write this poem."

BUTTER

In order to create each air bubble
between the layers of a croissant,
butter must be thinned out
inside the savoury dough
before melting away in the oven.
The butter disappears,
but you can still taste it.
When I disappear,
will anyone still taste me?

ABOUT THE POEM
"'Butter' is a simple and short piece about something I think about often: will anyone remember me when I'm gone? It's honestly that simple."

SQUID INK

There is a part of me that is squid ink black-
An empty so filled with darkness,
it doesn't ask for breath.
When my father reached blindly
for forgiveness
like a plump house cat for a dead mouse
I felt it swell.
When my mother emptied out
her sorrows
like yesterday's warm soda
down the drain
it told me to go to bed.
When my doctor baptized my ears

with condolences
without looking in my eyes
because he couldn't save my baby
I felt it fill me.

ABOUT THE POEM
"I wrote 'Squid Ink' because I really do feel a darkness in me that I can't explain. I dove into a couple moments or scenarios in my life where I felt this darkness, and at the end when I felt it 'fill me' I am implying being suicidal."

ABOUT JACQUELYN
Jacquelyn is 22 years old, and lives in Oregon, USA. She is happily married to her husband Nick, and are dog parents to a corgi Franklin. She writes poetry because it provides a space for her thoughts to become art; no matter how positive or negative the thoughts are. She has been writing poetry since she was 12 years-old, and since then been in love and have had wonderful teachers and mentors who have helped her find my voice; she would not be writing today without their support and guidance.
E: jacquelyncla@hotmail.com

Poetry by A.H. Waterfall

DEATHS FRUIT

Once, I did desire death,
I wished for its tantalizing taste,
Although it did remain at bay
By my ever-cursed breath.

I would sit so stilly
As blithe shapes moved softly by,
Murmuring, under rusty streetlamps in the cold late hours,
To the Moon, might this be our last Goodbye?

But when the time came
For me to sink into her lasting embrace
I found myself wishing to flee
Realizing that dark peace was not for me.

So it was that desperate whimpers filled the nights
Yet were covered by Twilight's song
As all good things stayed behind closed doors, warm beds,
Far from the blinding of darkness's throng.

Once, I watched as the Moon moved on
To shine her light on those wise enough to see
Then feeling as the light slipped quietly away
Knowing now that her gentle touch was not for me.

ABOUT THE POEM
"I wrote this piece of work based on personal reflections concerning my sister's experiences and struggles with mental health, and the impacts that isolation had on her."

ABOUT A.H. WATERFALL
A.H. Waterfall resides in Melbourne, Australia, and is currently a young student.

Poetry by Joseph A. Farina

BRIDGE

has he lived the life
he sees before him
watching the river flow below
does he see the world
differently from this height
as he stands upon the ledge
that shall be eternally his

how do his thoughts interchange
from desire to despair
has he tasted hell
is darkness a rapture
that feeds his need

does he stand, alone,
above a chastised world
seeing it in true colours
does he feel the warm wind
as his eyes in their spiral trance
in fleeting flight
reach out to nothing
his dreams, his words
shattered
upon the uncaring
river below

SUICIDE CLUB

we were all
dark
brooding poets
with bandaged wrists
and sneers
survivors
of our holocaust
wrists self tattooed
by blue Gillettes
iconoclastic dreamers
with airs of apathy

scratching syntax
exploring words
so absolute
we touched infinity -
quoted "howl" and "kerouac"
experienced
exemption, in their
        vision -
post modern hamlets
dripping pathos
seeking our redemption
made love to ink-stained pages
spent evening with ourselves
read
only by
pubescent girls
escaping from
their bourgeois world
as we
sought
to impugn it ...

ABOUT JOSEPH
Joseph is a retired lawyer living in Ontario, Canada. Drawing from his profession, and his Sicilian-Canadian background, he is an internationally award winning poet, and his work appears in a large number of international publications, journals and anthologies.
E: jfarina@cogeco.ca

Poetry by Mónika Tóth

I CARRY MY BURDEN

I carry my burden,
my shame, my hate,
 all across my heart.
I carry my burden ,
my upset,my angry,
all across my soul.
in every seasons my worth,
my strength, my pain,
becomes less.
I want to suicide

MY THOUGHTS

This is my thoughts every day
I feel suicide is the answer
to many questions
it hides in side of me
suicide is sneaky

I DON'T LIKE MY LIFE

no colour,
no smile,
no love,
no hope,
I am staggered in darkness,
my hands start to tremble,
my body start to tremble,
I feel so useless,
I don't like my life,
I WANT TO SUICIDE.

ABOUT MÓNIKA
Mónika graduated in Humanities, and then studied accountancy. She is interested in culture, reading, painting, philosophy, photography, and international literature.
E: monikatoth314@yahoo.com
FB: @monika.toth.1422

Nila K. Bartley's story

Suicide. What an ugly word. It reared its gruesome head as if to strike. I could see it's huge fangs as it grinned at me as if to say I was no match for suicide. It laughed at me. The sound curdled my blood. I gave up and plunged the knife into my chest. I tried again. The wound was not very deep. I tried again. The knife was dull. The only knife in the kitchen at the group home and it was dull. However, it was still sharp enough to draw blood.

I stepped outside the women's restroom and another woman screamed. I looked down at myself. I had blood on my top and pants. I was also still holding the knife. No wonder, the woman screamed. It was not a sight they were used to ar the Portsmouth Public Library in Portsmouth, Ohio in 2007.

I really don't remember anything after that until I reached the local hospital. I kept peeking out of the door of my room. A man who was part of security at the hospital would continually yell at me as I would look out my door. I also remember when they advised me I would be going back to the Veterans Affairs (VA) hospital in Chillicothe, Ohio, my heart dropped in my chest. I didn't want to be committed there again.

I fervently wished my suicide attempt had been successful. Why did I want to end my own life? Because of the disease of paranoid schizophrenia, which had plagued me for several years already. I was very delusional. I thought I was the only human being on the planet and everyone else was part of a master race. The master race was using me for entertainment. They were all actors and actresses in this play they had written. And on my birthday, this master race was going to transform me into a worm.

To say that I was terrified was an understatement. And when you combine terrified with hopelessness, what ensues next is constant absolute fear. No joy. No smiles. No laughter. Then suicide seems the only way of escape from the continual turmoil within.

As I was transferred to the Veterans Affairs hospital in Chillicothe, Ohio, I was sure that the play was continuing, and the master race was having a good laugh at my expense. I remember asking one the medical staff riding in the back of the ambulance with me if worms could see or were blind. I cried. I thought I would never feel the sun on my face again. I would never feel what it like to be hugged again. I would never have an intelligent conversation again. On my birthday I would be turned into a worm, yet still have the intelligence of a human. And I would never experience any of those things again. This is from where my hopelessness had emerged.

I had already made up my mind that I was going to try

suicide again. I had thought it through and was convinced the master race could not subvert the law of gravity. I was going to jump off a high building or bridge and end my life that way.

While I was thinking all this out, I had been in the VA psych ward for several days already. The first 24 hours I was on suicide watch. A member of the VA staff was with me at all times. After that, I was released from suicide watch and given a room in the general population within the ward. I was very docile. After all, I didn't want to raise the master race's suspicions.

The VA doctors advised me they wanted me to try a new anti-psychotic called Risperdal. At this point, I didn't care and just nodded my head yes. What compelled me to be docile was the fact, as I have mentioned earlier, was that I had made up my mind to kill myself by jumping off a high building or bridge. I was just bidding my time until being released from the psych ward.

Meanwhile, I started noticing things that puzzled me. Some of the VA staff were listening to me with concern and compassion. One woman in particular was very caring. Why? Why would someone from the master race do this? I was confused as I pondered this. Other VA staff were non-caring, some were even mean, which just strengthen my paranoia and delusion. Also, I had been taking Risperdal for five weeks.

The VA located me to another group home after I was released from the psych ward. This one was in Chillicothe. Something was happening to me that I couldn't explain. Some of the employees at the group home would listen to me for long periods of time about my delusion. That coupled with the fact that some of the VA staff had also been kind was tearing down the wall of delusion. The light of reality was shining through the cracks that were now in that wall. This went on for about another four to six weeks.

One morning, I woke up and looked at where the seemly impenetrable wall of delusion had been. It was no more. The wall was gone. There was now only light and beauty. I no longer believed I was going to be transformed into a worm on my birthday. Just in the nick of time. Because it was already the middle of August, and my birthday was only about a month away. If I hadn't become convinced by those caring and compassionate people, I would have tried to kill myself again.

Never underestimate the power of being kind and compassionate. Because of some caring VA staff and group home employees, I am alive. I believe God put them in my life, as well as Risperdal being administered to me at the same time. It was all part of His greater plan. I am thankful to those caring people and to God. At present, I am stable and living a life of contentment, fulfilment, purpose and peace. Be kind to people with mental illness.

ABOUT THE PIECE
"This short personal story is about when I tried to commit suicide in 2007. I was very delusional, and because of my delusions, I was terrified all the time. Paranoid schizophrenia had made my life unbearable. I just wanted to end the fear that was with me everyday. My husband, (Jason) and I are both paranoid schizophrenics. We also both have the writing gift. By the grace of God, we are now both stable and have been for many years. At one time we were both delusional. We try and raise awareness about what it is like to be mentally ill. We also want to give hope to others in the same situation that there is a brighter tomorrow."

THE PORTAL

The portal to my soul, who can go there?
for this is where--
Where I keep all the secrets from the present and the past,
hoping into the future that they do not last.
To view these secrets through the portal you must travel,
I keep the portal shut tight as the secrets make my life unravel.
Who? Who can stop this? These secrets are my burden to bear,
what I would not do to rid myself of them,
and live a life free without care.
The portal to my soul, O God, I pray,
I am afraid to let anyone in and stay.
The secrets make my soul ugly and dark--
black as night,
who can fill my soul again with light.
I dare not look too far into the depths of my soul,
I feel I will go crazy and lose all control.
My mind and soul are on the precipice of madness,
despair I feel-- much more than overwhelming sadness.
The only answer to this despair is to end this misery and close the portal,
how I wish the Almighty would just take the secrets from this mortal.

ABOUT NILA
Nila lives in Ohio, USA with her forever love and husband, Jason. She is in her late fifties and has been stable for many years. Nila serves God and people by volunteering at her church. She hopes all who read her poems and short stories are blessed by them.
E: klaibernila@gmail.com

Poetry by Sazma Samir

SUICIDE ANNIVERSARY

The anniversary was here
I set the table with rusted silver
and porcelain chipped plates.
I feel the familiar cold shiver
The smell of rain follows him –
that fresh smell of grass and autumn.
I smile politely and lead him
to the table where fish bones lay.
With harsh crunches I swallow.
Wash it down quickly,
embrace the metallic aftertaste.
He speaks only in whispers –
a calm, low tone.
We watch the city fall asleep.
And I know what comes next.
He stands beside me, offering wilted tulips
Wrapping his cloak around me,
I am reminded of the edge of the building.
The wind, the city lights, the decision.
He pulls away, and I realise
I no longer crave his touch.
His lingering cold kiss faded
and I finally felt the heat of life.
He smiles a knowing smile
as he disappears into mist.
Next year, he would be back
and like today, I will welcome him.
The memory never really goes away
but soon it will become bearable.

ABOUT THE POEM
"A lot is spoken of the actual suicide attempt, but very little about the aftermath. Every month that passes is a win, every year is another year I pushed past all that got me to that point. I initially wrote 'Suicide Anniversary' when I had reached a year since my attempt and from then on, I have continued to make edits to it every year. I'm happy to say I plan to make many more edits in the future. This poem describes my relationship with death, the way he has become an old friend and the way I don't want his company as much as before. It is the culmination of my healing."

SURVIVAL

We've been in this pit before.
And we've crawled out on our hands and knees.
Scraping our palms on open rocks
till we bled warm blood.

We've been in this pit before.
The light outside the cave, our only hope.
Surrounded by nothing but darkness.
An endless abyss of which fear lived.

We've been in this pit before.
Sat in the silence of the void.
The only sound; the hum of our blood gushing
and the gnawing of the monsters on our heels.

We've been in this pit before.
And we crawled out alive.

ABOUT THE POEM
"While struggling with mental illness, I created this reminder of how I could survive the current moment because I had survived the past moments. At the time I was struggling with familial problems and felt as though I could only rely on myself. Hence, having a rehearsed phrase kept me alive. Survival is than mantra I repeated to myself every day to get through every harsh thought, instinct, and bad habit."

COPING MECHANISM

Flesh split apart hastily
The blade dull from use.
Maroon ink seeps out,
a stream of consciousness
finding its way onto the page.
The pain forms its own words,
staining the side of my left hand
as I empty my brain onto the page.
Squeeze my right arm to urge more.
Head spinning with every letter
but it cannot be stopped.
The poison must come out.
Finally, the bleeding stops.

Skin now paper white,
I can sleep for now.
Until I feel the poison enter again.

ABOUT THE POEM
"For the longest time, writing was my only solace. It created a space for me to release my emotions in a manner that did not hurt me. The good and the bad in my life became my inspiration to create something beautiful, but haunted. But as issues persisted, I found myself melding writing with the darkest coping mechanisms. Using these terrible methods as some form of release became my new inspiration and in return, my writing became a perpetuating factor in my self-harm. For a long time I thought I couldn't be a creative without the pain but I believe that is the biggest lie the world has ever sold to me."

GHOSTS

The smile feels natural now.
The bright one, the mask melting
into my skin and mind.
The bright lights numb the darkness.
The drink numbs the mind.
And in that haze, I vaguely see
the ghost of the person I used to be.

The low feels normal now.
When the night is done
and I'm finding my way back.
The feeling of returning to gravity.
No longer able to float.
I miss seeing myself in the mirror.
Take me back to the lights.

ABOUT THE POEM
"Self-harm is something that comes in many forms. One of the ways it came to me was in the form of numbing myself in any way possible. And in my generation, what might be seen as fun can very easily be used in a terrible way. The vices some of us carry are so easily camouflaged in plain sight – alcoholism disguised as a partier, risky sex disguised as confidence, and the list goes on. It is a terrifying and shocking realisation for so many, including me. When I realised what I had been doing, I wrote 'Ghosts'. I'd love to say that with the realisation came a sudden stop to this form of self-harm.

Unfortunately, self-harm is an addiction and I still sometimes struggle with relapsing."

SHOWER DRAIN

My shower drain is clogged.
Something crowds the tube,
forcing water to drain slowly.
It trickles down through the pipes.
I kept the surface clean.
Holes polished; hair removed.
And yet the drain clogged.

I ignore it as I shower once more.
Matted hair smoothed out.
Loofa scraping dirt and sweat away.
Daisy soap to hide the smell.
I swish the excess water between my toes.
Watching the ripples clash.
The splash as the soap mixes in.

I swish more water to the drain.
The excess threatens to overflow.
I worry of the soapy footprints it'll leave.
Too obvious of a mess to hide.
Unlike the scars under my clothes.
The soap circles the drain
but none go in.

I want to unclog my shower drain.
But nothing works.
No drain cleaner, no acid pour.
The dirt had crusted, solidified.
Years of use had left it tough.
Peering into pristine holes,
I dare lift the veil.
The darkness mirrors me.

My shower drain is clogged.
My final stand, bare and shivering,
I venture down the abyss.
The mess. The stickiness.
My nails claw, raw and bloody.
Swish the water at my feet

but there's none left to sweep.

ABOUT THE POEM
"It is easy to look at someone who seems to be doing better as completely healed, when in reality there is so much more to dig out. This poem was written recently when I realised that despite pulling myself away from many bad coping mechanisms, I still had so much more to clean out. Many habits and thoughts have dried and fused with me. But I will no longer let that continue. I have to clean it out slowly, no matter how gross and messy it may be. Because I deserve better."

UNIQUE

We compared scars like they were player cards
Sized each other's burns in the mirror
proclaiming who had it worse
as we ignored the burning house.
Like medals we paraded our broken pieces,
Exchanging trauma around campfire
and laughing at the faces of our horrors.
We thought it made us special to have been hurt.
Our trophies were ashes with our home
and all we had were ourselves.

ABOUT THE POEM
"When I finally met others like me, when I realised that it wasn't me alone suffering, I thought I found some form of family. Instead I found that we seemed to revel in our suffering; like it made us special. Our traumas are not what makes us special, and yet we compared it like any of us could actually win that competition. But I understood why; that desperate attempt to give reason to all the pain – from others and self-inflicted. If we could create a reason, the suffering could be justified. Despite all this, somewhere in that competition, I did find compassion and laughter in the darkness."

ABOUT SAZMA
Sazma is a 20 year-old Singaporean writer. She was born in India before promptly moving to Singapore with her parents, and is now studying in the University of Wollongong, Australia. At 16, she published her first book after four years of work. Her writing style continues to evolve and grow, branching out from the Fantasy-Fiction genre to poetry and short prose, thanks to the influence of her love for literature cultivated in classrooms during her secondary years.

Her poetry is deeply influenced by modern issues, as well as her own experiences as a young adult in chaotic times, and ranges from the emotions of a teenager to issues she advocates for.
E: sazma2002@gmail.com
Instagram: @thenovicewriter_

Poetry by Joan McNerney

I PLANTED MY GARDEN

on the wrong side
of moon forgetting
tides of ocean
lunar wax wane

only madness
was cultivated
there underground
tubular roots
corpulent veins

flowers called
despair gave off
a single fruit...

I ate it
my laughter
becoming harsh
my eyes grew
oblique

ABOUT THE POEM
"This is when the anxiety and anger started to grow."

I AM JUNK

dirty city dirty junk
once i was useful
passed from 1 hand
to another dragged
thru his desire & hers
pushed down

who threw me here
putting a needle of
lead in my brain?
lead completely then
left thrown on this dump
a piece of leaden junk

how long will i
lie here lie here
the heroin/e?
with heavy body
full round sobs
cold hideous
why can't i cry out?

ABOUT THE POEM
"This is when I felt hopeless and useless because I could not study at university."

SUICIDE SNEAKS

thru blue bedroom, a chair
falls across bedspread
spins along random floor
i wander up wall, hang
suspended from light bulb

phone rings we speak into
plastic wire did you know
how dizzy i am i am i am
in bathroom blushing curtains
razor blades near sink
now polishing scarred
vanity table, cut in my arm
how white!

ahhh *furnishedbluebedroom*
insides of *existentialessays*
televisionscreens
perfectpatchesofcement
boxes boxes boxes
something hiding important
under coils in back of brain
only this makes me happy
insects busy night&day
i hear them.

ABOUT THE POEM
"I came from a dysfunctional family and no one seemed to care about me. I left home when still in high school. My friends all had better

home lives, but none of them could really help me. It was upsetting to see people with less talent and brains go off to college while I was stuck waiting tables in New York City. Anxiety and anger caused me to go off the rails. I never actually tried committing suicide, but did consider it as an option during many long and lonely nights."

ABOUT JOAN
Joan has been the recipient of three scholarships. She has recited her work at the National Arts Club, New York City, State University of New York, Oneonta, McNay Art Institute, San Antonio and the University of Houston, Texas, as well as other distinguished venues. A reading in Treadwell, New York was sponsored by the American Academy of Poetry, and four Best of the Net nominations have been awarded to her. She has published two collections: *The Muse in Miniature* and *Love Poems for Michael,* and her work has been published in literary publications too numerous to mention in over thirty five countries worldwide. Joan has just released is a new title *At Work*. This collection shows colorful but realistic snapshots of working women and men in their daily lives.
E: poetryjoan@statetel.com

Poetry by Biswajit Mishra

WHO CAN TELL WHY?

Running into friends away from home,
just an acquaintance seems closer,
distance of places inversely correlates with
intimacy and at one gathering in a place in the
land of dreams, a visitor arrives uninvited,
tagging along to another, sees many—
some new, some old, some just known faces
who might have hung out in the same college
in different companies; many seem settled,
some settling, some trying to make it — mostly
young families, and one of them introduces
his beautiful wife who is in the family way —
small talks, stray reminiscing of some common
strands, an evening well spent, oceans away.

A few years down,
the visitor hears from his friend about
another gathering filled with happy guests,
happier hosts for the child's birthday, the
hospitable hostess swirling around, bubbling,
like a songbird, checks with each to make sure
they are having a good time, makes sure foods
keep flowing as do the drinks, old buddies and
their families hang out late, as usual, a few may
have been slithering down in their seats rebelling
against the five days of slavery to their watches—
fully reliant upon the verbal and physical tugging
from their better halves, and after they are gone,
the din has flattened out, a calmness descends,
fatigue wakes to show its might, yet the hostess
cleans up, asks her family to go sleep as she goes
about putting the house back to order, perhaps
resetting it to its primordial state where
potential would have its full chance,

and in the quietness detached from drunken stupor,
a void rises out of smoke from the smouldering
woods which might have been seeped in a wetness
that rains from the sky have nothing to do with,
nor the sun of the sky has ever seen to dry them.

A quiet house,
almost dark house,
almost the wee hours:
why does the sun take long to wake up,

why do the rains take time drenching,

why is the cool breeze of the evening tardy,

why the smoke keeps snarling —a snake
from a different garden lures the silent bird
into the depths of non-echoes,

why she leaves mixing up her homes, and

why she chooses to board the rail-tracks
instead of a train and leaves an empty house
stripped of its home?

ABOUT BISWAJIT
Biswajit writes poems predominantly in English and sporadically in his native Indian language Odia. His poems have appeared in the poetry magazines *The Year of the Poet*, *Indian periodical,* and *The Poet.* He is currently working on a collection by aiming to write at least one poem per day over 365 days. His subjects are varied and include nature, animals, plants, spiritual concepts, families, and travel experiences.
E: biswajitpoetry@gmail.com
FB: @Biswajit Mishra
Instagram: @biswajitmishra.ig
Twitter: @Biswajitca

Poetry by Francis Muzofa

ME

I miss You,
I terribly miss You,
I didn't know it was going to be this terrible,
I miss my young,
I miss my younger self,
The energy,
The innocence,
The ambition,
The fearlessness,
The risks slayed,
The mountains climbed,
The flooded rivers crossed,
The David and Goliath fights fought,
I miss that guy,
That guy,
I am miserable,
I am spent,
My brain is shrinking by the hour,
My muscles are not spared,
My zeal is sold,
My marrow very narrow,
My eyesight short,
My ears angled wrongly,
The sharpness is gone,
Life is winning me,
It's kicking me in the loins,
The referee is not interested,
Should I throw in the towel?
Should I use it to wipe my sweat?
Or to cover my scars,
I seriously need motivation,
My coach is lost,
This ring ain't friendly,
None is,
The coach,
The referee,
The opponent,
The audience,
They all want me butchered,
Even the universe seem to be conniving,

I am losing it,
If only I could awaken that guy,
The guy who knew no defeat,
The guy who was always optimistic,
The guy who always had a plan,
The guy with determination,
The guy who always had deep oases,
Of wisdom,
Of strength,
Of foresight,
I miss that guy,
That guy,
My younger self,
The dynamite
May be it exploded too early,
Now the enemies are here,
Should I take my life?
Should I take away with my life?
Before they take my life,
Is it worth saving after all?
Cornered in a corner,
I am cornered
Life!
I betrayed life,
If not, life betrayed I,
Wasted vacation,
Heaven too only takes highly confident people,
Not people who take their own life,
Looks like by a thread,
I will hang,
Between heaven and earth,
Life!

ABOUT THE POEM
"I wrote the poem 'Me' more for myself, given how I am changing with age; I can't do what I used to do with ease. However this poem is national, given how I see my family members and others my age struggling to make ends meet, especially with the economic challenges Zimbabwe has been going through for the past two decades. Age and economic situation is conniving to harm the people. Most parents in their 40s and above are finding it extremely difficult to manage their basic financial obligations, leaving them with suicidal thoughts or, at worst, actually committing suicide."

ABOUT FRANCIS

Francis is a published poet from Namibia and Zimbabwe. He has published both locally and internationally. He enjoys writing wisdom poetry, where he normally employs satire or allegory to address some of the national and global challenges; health, climate, nature and social issue are his favourite hunting ground, with his pen his best hunting dog *"It's very powerful; it can even take down elephants."*
Twitter: @MuzofaFrancis

Norman Morrissey's story

PREFACE TO ST MARK'S DIARY

These poems were sketched in Saint Mark's Psychiatric Clinic, East London [South Africa], in the waxing of the Easter moon, the 1st to the 11th of April, 2003, Days 13 to 23 of the Iraqi War. I was working through a breakdown, doing cold turkey on years of sleeping pills and painkillers, and at last getting full clinical diagnosis on a condition that began with an infection, trashing my nervous system in November, 1962, a month after my 13th birthday.

As far as I can understand it, endogenous depression is a psycho-physical state in which signals being transmitted within nerves in the brain are impeded, weakened in strength and clarity, because the body isn't producing enough serotonin.

Serotonin is the neurohormone that works within the spaces between contiguous nerve cells – in the synaptic clefts – to make the information embodied in incoming signals carry through the nerve to be processed by the brain as sensory experience. For me, endogenous depression has been what I imagine a malfunctioning sensory deprivation chamber would feel like: you get the world – and your own bodily sensations – screened and filtered down to a set of minimalist clues. You get a trickle, when you should naturally have a stream.

My memory of walking out of hospital in such depression was like finding someone had broken the aerial so the sound and picture were fuzzed, pale shadows of themselves before I got sick. There just wasn't enough power in my impressions for them to elicit natural responses. The feeling of reality to the senseworld was gone, texture and timbre were no longer activated as live sensations, it was like having the world behind grimy plate-glass and my body somewhere in another room: try running Concorde on Zippo fuel.

Like any animal with its senses on the blink, part of the natural response to such a close-down is a dramatic increase in the body's production of adrenalin – the fight or flight trigger – which is experienced as chronic, nameless anxiety that in time burns down to chronic anxious fatigue. This works with your impaired quantity and quality of spontaneous awareness – awareness which isn't driven by willpower – to drastically reduce your ability to concentrate on anything except the distress circuiting your own psychic system. At times of real environmental pressure, you can be debilitated almost to standstill: when I wrote my Honours exams in February, 1973, for the past five months I hadn't been able to read more than three or four pages in a single, four-four stint of work. I, at last, burned out through stress and, what was for me, over-work in March, 2001. I landed in St Mark's two years later, when I'd finally got all the mechanics of my disability retirement settled so my family were as financially secure as I could make them. (Depressives are often terrible plodders).

These poems are part of the habit I've formed of using poetry to fill and round the gaps in my natural resources. I discovered Yeats's *Sailing to Byzantium* when I was 18, and the poem was a revelation and a confirmation in one: the aged soul, that "must louder sing/ For every tatter in its mortal dress" made immediate sense of my condition. Each poem I've managed since has been a bit of "the artifice of eternity" that I can use to magpie the roof of my soul. To the extent to which a poem "works" – is true to its first promptings but can still speak to other people authentically – my experience gains a depth of meaning it doesn't very often have as it happens to me. I almost always get the joke late.

Most of the poems featured below were written or sketched while I was too tired to think straight, in too much physical pain to sleep, and afraid of tipping into pits even deeper than the one in which I sincerely tried suicide. (As Hopkins said of another context of spiritual stress, the mind has "cliffs of fall/ No man measured"; you can reach "no worst/ There is none", simply because the deeper you've fallen, the deeper you can go: despair is a downward curve of learning, a function of diseased imagination. Spike Milligan described the down-swing as an endless corridor, doors closing behind you as others open ahead, each another balk away from sanity).

And John Clare in his early 19th Century asylum – who "wrote till earth was but a name" – was almost terribly real to me. The poems that he made in such numbers (that allowed him to be "undistrest" however "friendless" he was) stood for me as fixed stars of immense courage and sanity. He fabricated – with the only materials available to him – poised crystals, each made out of memories, and from an innate lovingness that must often have had desperately little in his immediate experience of his circumstances to feed it. I had the promise of the best proven treatments, Clare didn't even have the beginnings of an understanding of his malady – probably bipolar disorder, the old-style manic-depressive condition – that might have brought him a touch of earthly hope. I am very glad to be living in the 21st Century.

When I say that these poems were "sketched" in the Clinic, I mean they've been put through whatever amendment any of them might have needed to remove clumsiness and obscurities I would have corrected at the time of writing - if I'd recognized them then. "Composition" comes from "to compose": to settle your words into the manner natural to their fullest and deepest original purposes.

Since what we do is always coloured by unconscious and semi-conscious motives, composing a poem into its true voice can take a good deal of time, and the exercise of a lot of humble and practised self-examination. A term you grab in the rush of free-writing is often just a shorthand label you later need to test and articulate into an image. The pressure of intuitions can sometimes make you poise a word or line wrongly, so it clashes with the real texture of feeling and of thought the poem is actually dramatizing: you need Sherlock Holmes, and you've got Mike Hammer – or worse, vice versa.

For me, a poem must speak. Long before any extractable ideas it may have in mind, it has to have a person to whom those thoughts are happening – it must be the impress of that person's mind and of the ply of felt and intuited awarenesses that at any moment make up a mind. And being depressive by long physical bent, I take time to be able to read what I can of the feelings complexing and event together. Beyond its normal need in serious writing, editing is also part of my strategy in trying to be emotionally literate; for me to "write up" or falsify – rather than honestly access what I can of my felt subtext – would be psychic death. The mystery of awareness starts more obviously close to my doorstep than it seems to with people who are more naturally quick with felt knowledge.

What I have done with these poems is to see that they come as near as I can get them to sounding like the moods their thoughts grew in – which is far from being the same as simply having the words in which the first impressions of the thoughts sketched themselves for me. Even with pristine synapses, you are always only very partially aware of the breaking story of your own intuitions and responses, so self-editing is a function of self-knowledge, not an evasion or falsifying.

The sequence in which the poems are presented is that in which they were written.

5

The place is so quiet
you say, waiting to go home, we the only ones left from last week,
                      me saying:
It's like a tomb!

Or like a church
I say as I pad about
religiously absorbed in my pain.

37

I think you should just come out and say it,
"I'm an alcoholic"
he said:

I must tell people, it's not a shame,
they need to understand for others who can't speak.

That's where you're disadvantaged, I said,
You're black, look at these broken veins in my nose,
I don't have to say
anything.

41

Forty years of depression
– and now it seems
time and treatment could really make a difference,
could make me more natural:

all those holy mountains I made
of such a molehill

– taking diseased nerves for spiritual obtuseness,
thinking I had poor will and shaky wits I must learn to discipline
when it was a silk purse I was wanting from a synaptic sow's ear;

but still,
if Hermes does pursue me down the desolate gulfs of Homer's
unharvested deep

– fish me up to the sun –

just warm sand
would be treasure.

57

Whatever gods there are,
this night
give me guidance,

give me wisdom to know the guidance,
give me courage to act on the wisdom,
I'm finished,
I can't take any more grind of sleeplessness and the voices of my stress
twisting more and more turns of the screw:

even if you don't really exist to listen
I do.

77

Poor Gilli, she pulls up,
finds me out in the sun to be fetched:

and you can see in her face
– those talks on the phone while I was in –
she wouldn't be shook to find me with a bolt through my neck
and a sign,

Connect 220 volts daily after meals.

ABOUT THE POEMS
"These poems are taken from 'St Mark's Diary', a collection of 80 poems, accompanied by a CD, which was written in St Mark's clinic when I was trying to heal from lifelong depression that caused me to try suicide. The poems share glimpses of the experience of being in a psychiatric clinic, and show the way in which the activity of writing poems can create stepping stones - like prayers - towards some sense of surviving, worthy self, however rudimentary it may be; a self who, as the 77th poem testifies, can even view itself ironically and elicit a wry grin or even a short guffaw from its reader. The poems were written during the Iraqi war, and many of them refer directly to that war, or more broad war themes. For this particular selection, however, I have excluded those poems in favour of ones that specifically target the process of inner damage and healing."
E: silkeheiss@gmail.com
W: www.silkeheiss.co.za
Blog: https://silkeheiss.blogspot.com
FB: @GiveYourWritingTheEdge

Prose by J. Robert Schott

PURGATORY

Purgatory is a place on the lower astral plane where lost souls sometimes go, or people who commit suicide. No matter what the Catholics say, babies do not go there if they are not baptized; that is a lie - they are faultless. Because people believe that suicide is a crime against God, they put themselves there. It is a hell of a place.

One time, in my long fifteen year depression, I tried to commit suicide; life was that bad. The people at the hospital kept working on me all night; pumping my stomach and breathing for me with a bag. I went to purgatory for a time. Everybody there was caught up in the same sad repetitive thoughts, going over them again and again ... ad infinitum. Nothing I could say could snap any of them out of it. A nice Mormon policeman who had come to my 911 call, sat outside my emergency cubicle all night praying for me. The doctors worked on into the night. Eventually around dawn they brought me back and I survived, but the memory of my narrow escape from purgatory stayed with me. For months afterward I still had one foot in limbo, and tortured souls from there were coming to me regularly looking for help. Nothing I could say could get them out of their repeating hellish thoughts. One of these souls was my ex-mother-in-law. I loved the woman. For days she plagued me with her tortured thoughts. Finally I asked the Mahanta, a spiritual guide, for help. He came in the light body and talked to her for a while. Then a great white-winged was being manifested to us, whom I did not recognize, but my mother-in-law did. She knew him from somewhere; her face lit with joy and she flew into his arms, and we never saw either of them again.

I told this story to my ex and she explained that my mother-in-law had committed suicide. My ex found the story very interesting.

The Yellow Hats of Tibet and the Mormons sometimes practice the rescue of lost souls; there may be others but unless someone intervenes, souls are stuck in limbo for an eternity. It is literally a hell of a place to go, and I gave up on suicide from that point ...

Poetry by Iona Winter (Waitaha)

BLACKBIRD

There is no shelter in this empty whare I've become, and the mamae — I hate the way that kupu contains 'mama'.

In the wind is the sound of my unvoiced keening; in the mama blackbird's beak the worms of my earthbound grief, and in the sunshine on my upturned face reminders of your tenderness.

I walk the in-between, accustomed to the piercing threat of losing myself to this sorrow. And I kid myself, that if I look deeply enough into my mirror-reflected eyes I might glimpse you there.

When will I emerge from my own shallow grave?

I wobbled last night at your second wake, and knew precisely how you'd joined the tupuna — to rest in the whetū, and lay your hands upon my back. But I no longer recognise the landscape of my body, like the ash that is weeping.

These tears dripping from chin to bare knees will never cease — the impermanence of life and permanence of death.

Tell me, where is the home for bereaved mothers?

Te Reo Māori words:
whare: house
mamae: pain
kupu: word
tupuna: ancestors
whetū: stars

First published with takahē Magazine (NZ), 2022.

AMPUTATED LIMBS

I walk in the deserted reserve, remembering our last time here,
And the lines on my belly that once held you close now shout, HE'S DEAD.

At the lightning-split tī kōuka I want to climb inside and rest awhile,
I'm so tired of this sadness.

Or should I head for the bowl formed in the hollow left by an amputated limb?
You know, the one where the kererū drink.

One broken branch appears like a hand held over my heart
Fingers curved in a caress, the wrist lichen-lined.

It is a surprise to see now that the sky also has a split —
Where light meets dark, and sun kisses the rain.

Te Reo Māori words:
tī kōuka: cabbage tree
kererū: wood pigeon

First published with *Verb and Katherine Mansfield House & Garden* (NZ), 2021.

ABOUT THE POEMS
"In 2020, my only child Reuben took his life, and he is the third grandchild in two years in our whānau (family) to suicide."

ABOUT IONA
Iona lives in Te Wai Pounamu, the South Island of Aotearoa, New Zealand, and is the author of three collections: *Gaps in the Light* (2021), *Te Hau Kāika* (2019), *then the wind came* (2018), and has recently completed her fourth. Skilled at voicing difficult topics, Iona is of mixed ancestry; Māori and European, and creates work that spans genre and form. Widely published and anthologised internationally, her poetry and hybrid fiction have been performed solo, and in collaboration with other multimedia artists. Iona holds a Master's degree in Creative Writing, is currently working on a creative non-fiction project addressing the complexities of being suicide bereaved. She is editor for *Elixir & Star Press*, a newly created and dedicated space for the expression of grief in New Zealand.
W: www.ionawinter.wordpress.com
FB: @IonaWinter11
Instagram: @iona_winter

Poetry by Lesley Warren

BLACK NIGHT SONNET

Until you have keened like a bird in a trap
rued the spark of your very conception
Stoppered your mouth and screamed into fists
bloodied from flying at walls
Begged for forgiveness from all you once loved
when you lived beyond mere respiration
Greeted the hateful black visitor who
returns and returns and returns
and each time believed his mock farewell
Heartsick at your failures
By despair so tightly shackled
All your treasures turned to ashes
Mutely loathing your existence
do not speak to me of pain.

ABOUT THE POEM
"'Black Night Sonnet' was a piece from 2019. I wanted to write in a more formal, almost Shakespearian voice to express my inner rage at the unfairness of suffering from mental illness. Depression is not something that everyone understands, but pain is, and this is what I tried to capture in this piece."

THE VESSEL OVERFLOWS

Sadness lives
in my shoulders.
I have long housed it there,
as worry chose the stomach for itself.

There isn't much of me,
my mortal shell.
Five feet, two inches
of tight-packed hell.

Compact. Dense.
And *tense*.
The well-worn face is bloated with emotion.

Have you ever harboured demons?

Jump ship. This vessel's set to overflow.

If *feel* is all I am
and *feel* is me
am I allowed to ache
allowed to bleed?

My own mind making worms' meat out of me.

What of *anger*?
A small black pocket in the heart
contains the taste of ashes.

ABOUT THE POEM
"I wrote 'The Vessel Overflows' on one of the many occasions when the mental burden of depression was weighing not only on my mind, but also on my physical body and my spirit. The enormity of the feeling of depression is sometimes overwhelming, and feels bigger than I am. However, I am a member of the ABCTales writing website. Reading this piece aloud at one of our regular virtual reading nights gave me a sense of catharsis and release."

NADIR
Most people grow up and grow wiser
Flourish, flock to one another
With their silly shiny smiles
But I metastasise, human tumour
Growing sick and warped and ugly
Draining life from all I touch.
I was born with hidden blackness
A single venomous seed
And when it finally took root
It erased the bright child I had been.
Now I'm making up for squandered years
Caught fast in tendrils black
Fantasising teen rebellion
Half a decade too late
Stumbling down the path to adulthood
With scabs on both my knees.
Why do I have to fight harder
Stretch my hand out that bit further
Jump that extra few feet higher
To snatch one fleeting gold moment
From the inky firmament?

Is there something I don't see?
Is it just because I'm me?
Building-block life
Tumbles grand into the dust
While I shield my ears from promises
That I no longer trust.
I want to produce things of beauty
Want a clean-snow-dove-white legacy
So no-one knows I've seen the world end
Every day for an eternity.
Why do I believe
The most alive I'd ever feel
Is if you put a gun up to my head
And told me to kneel?

25

It was my intention to die
On birthday (deathday) twenty-five
When the air was shrouded in winter's grey
February skies already clad for mourning
In a hotel haphazard home between non-homes
In a foreign land. Like a poet.
It would have been poignant and stoic.
I washed my hair and left my note
But ultimately
I added "Dying" to the long list of my failures.
Life is purgatory
And I hate that it's too much
And that I am not enough.
In spite of myself
I exist (on borrowed time?)
Tell myself I can bow low, exit stage right
Whenever I can really take no more
But something, something always makes me pause
At the threshold of that final welcome door.

ABOUT THE POEMS
"'Nadir' and '25' are two very dark pieces written during one of the most challenging periods of my life to date. I had recently moved from the UK to Germany to pursue my career, and it seemed to me that I had made a terrible decision. My boyfriend back in the UK had broken up with me, I had encountered racist harassment in Germany, and the accommodation I had signed a contract on before it was fully

built wasn't ready on the due date. The building company put me up in a bed and breakfast hotel in the middle of an industrial estate on the very outskirts of the city, far away from anything. Thus I spent my 25th birthday alone, friendless, surrounded by moving boxes in a foreign hotel room. The TV played only Spanish shows. I did not speak Spanish. Thankfully things got much better for me, but it did take its sweet time."

NIGHT WALK HAIKU

heart is hollowed out
would serve a better purpose
as my soul's ashtray

ABOUT THE POEM
"'Nght walk haiku' is a very recent piece that came to me as I walked home in the dark. I had gone out for no reason other than wanting to be away from the house. Really, I wanted to be less trapped inside myself, and thought physical movement would help. I felt useless and hopeless. The cars rushed under me as I crossed the overpass, their lights ephemeral in the darkness. As I walked past the hospital where I had spent three weeks after a mental breakdown during the pandemic, the following haiku formed out of the crisp night air."

SLEEP IS FOR THE WEAK

Sleep, they say, is for the weak
and I am weak
but I can't sleep.
I'm running on frenetic dreams
Held together by caffeine seams
and other people's expectations
in between skyscraper gleams
The morning bet as I down my joe:
tunes my brain in like a radio
or traps me in that hazy horror
tense fight-or-flight, paranoia
hearing colours, tasting time.
I'm in that crazy no man's land
Performing daily miracles
Sickening for something
Cartwheeling over obstacles
Forgetting my own name

With ecstatic heart
Leaden eyes
Unfettered soul
and a cloud compacted in my head.
If I can just push though these gates
wade through the black floodwaters
there's the land of dervish typing
and fevered ins/expiration
But this place here's just the station
with just one train running daily
Going straight to Failureville. (Population: you).
Life's a drug, it consumes you
Life lives you and it dooms you
And you can't hop off
You can't take a breather
You can't save your place.
Oh God please
let me not exist, just for a while.
But wilful life's covering its ears and going LA LA LA
Sprinting to the abyss
Relentlessly, carelessly, sadistically
it just keeps
going.
Until
one day
it

s
t
o
p
s.

ABOUT THE POEM
"'Sleep Is For The Weak' came to me like a bolt from the blue. I was exhausted and unable to turn off my mind's chatter, struggling to meet the demands imposed upon me by the daily commute and nine to five office job, social life, errands and my mental health. Getting the words down in a frenzy of typing helped me release some tension."

ABOUT LESLEY
Lesley lives for language. She was born to British and Filipino parents and works as a translator in Germany. Her ongoing struggle with

depression casts a long shadow, but also fuels the darker side of her creative output. Typical themes of her poetry and prose, which have been featured in numerous online and print anthologies, include the search for identity, trauma and "otherness".
Instagram: @lem246
Twitter: @LifeofLem
YouTube: @LIFE OF LEM

Poetry by John Tunaley

A WARNING DREAM
(Skating On Thin Ice)

Skating on thin ice, I lose my balance,
and my stovepipe hat. Too elaborate
by far ... my flying swirls...swooping ornate
pirouettes ... CRASH! I'm forced to change my stance

I stoop my shoulders, stare at the near ground,
(not gaze into the impervious sky).
I concentrate on having gravity...
... spread stubby arms, waddle round and around
like a grandfather penguin and then halt ...
What a transformation! From spell binding
acrobat to bag of rags shuffling
up a dead-end street. I can summersault
no more. There's a freezing-white pitiless full moon ...
... she's seen it all before. I rock sideways ... move on ...

HOPELESSNESS
(Alabama Fudge Cake)

It's a funny old business ...'Hopelessness'.
Waterlogged, my submarine had surfaced,
and although it wallowed down in the troughs,
my sad-angled periscope's smeared cross wires
caught my miserable, weak, attention ...
Something prompted me to scan the cake names,
(It's been months since I'd ...'Exhausted the List').

Half-heartedly squinting at written tags...
'Alabama Fudge' stopped me in my tracks.
How long had the cake stood there, unnoticed
by my blindfolded soul's world weariness?
It helped me to fight back ... re-energise ...
... save my wasp from the spider's softly silent rush,
... divert my beetle from the boot fall's threatened crush ...

ABOUT JOHN
John was born in Manchester in 1945. Father: foundry hand, mother;
crane-driver is what his birth certificate states ... (the war was a

melting pot ... throwing them together at the steel works). He now lives in Robin Hood's Bay, North Yorkshire. He's in a few writing groups ... (Natalie keeps the Whitby Library Writing Group blog up to date ... it's too tricky for John). He sticks to sonnets, as the form exercises some control of his worst excesses. They pile up ... the excesses ... He likes anthologies ... he enjoys the company ... (and there's safety in numbers ...).
E: johntunaley@yahoo.co.uk

Poetry by Til Kumari Sharma

PREVENTING SUICIDE WITH POETRY

The reading poetry gives me hope.
The aspiration is born from beauty of words.
Alienation is positive by reading lines.
The hope of life is poetry.

It prevents to go to grave.
Even grave is defeated by artistic words.
The suicide is the messy game.
Never enter in suicidal action.
Read and write words and weave garland of art.

Poetry is healing method not to go in death.
Life is blooming there.

Words prevent suicide

ART AS OUR ETERNAL HOME

Art kills our mental trauma.
The divinity of words cleans our mental illness.
The divine words rob the dirt of my mind.
Then words and art clean the mental tension.
The divinity of words is from insanity.
That is creative to rub the tension and worries.
Then the words make my eternal home.
The artistic pain is creative enough.
I am healed and happy then.
I feel relief in these art of writing.

Art is eternal life.

MEDICAL WAVES

Writing as thoughtful emotion
To share pain and wound
Like soul mate to care
Writing helps to share pain

Words are like medical waves
To make me survival to bring good health
Words are our weapons to heal wound
They are like medical waves

Words make minds healthy

ABOUT THE POEMS
"I felt previously as an isolated person, not loved by other, but now I can heal others because my words make me strong and independent. My words are in me to kill negative thoughts. So words are healing sources of life. The words make me busy enough to write the artistic light, that saves me and my consciousness. Words pause suicide."

ABOUT TIL
Also known as Pushpa, Til was born in Parbat, West Nepal. She was not allowed to study for her PhD in her own country, so she went to India to study. She has published over 6000 poems and 180 essays and other literary works.
E: authortilkumarisharma@gmail.com
Blog: www.tilaism-pushpaism.blogspot.com

Poetry by Antoni Ooto

DEPRESSION'S TUNNEL

with first steps fitting my feet
into long-worn tracks
cold wraps in sweat

my heart hammers
and pills that fight apathy
erase joy

staring left, staring right,
(which way? which way?)
trying to move yet frozen

in time
night becomes days
days become years

just move, move

ahead, one light...
darkness losing its grip

a chance to turn
one hundred eighty degrees
to follow tracks
that lead to a better story

a story of change
move, move

       I've tried.

ABOUT ANTONI
Based in New York, USA, Antoni's work is widely published globally in print, online, and in anthologies. His poems reflect special memories, a love of nature, and the listening to life's smaller moments. He is also a well-known abstract expressionist artist whose paintings are collected throughout the US.
E: antoniotoart@gmail.com
Linkedin: @antoniooto

Poetry by Judy DeCroce

WALKING ON

A twist of time
one seagull
one turning between tides.

Now, I, an empty shack,
push a pain too close to keep.

Scout wanders the shore
watches pale leftover prints in sand.

~

He was just a man, not a sailor lost at sea
and said —
this time would be different

but there hid a sweeping depression
falsely tamed.

Now here we are—
      a dog with loyalty...
           me with love.

It didn't matter.

First appeared in *OPEN: Journal of Arts & Letters*, Winter/2020.

ABOUT JUDY
Based in New York, USA, Judy is an internationally published poet, flash fiction writer, and recently published *The Posture Of Trees*, a book of poetry with her husband, Antoni Ooto. This year her poem, *One Woman Leads to Another,* was nominated for the Pushcart Prize. She is also a professional storyteller, and teacher of that genre, as well as offering courses in flash fiction.
E: judydecroce@yahoo.com
LinkedIn: @JudyDeCroce

Poetry by Hasanul Hoq

I CAME BACK

I can't but forget that moment,
Happened many times in my life,
I was nearly convinced to fall in love in detaching the soul and body;
I started, I was thinking about my family, my life, sweet memories,
I cried silently,
Death was calling me, I was spreading my hands;
I came back.

ABOUT THE POEM
"*As a human, we are brave by birth. I did the same thing while facing suicidal attempts. My experiences helped me to come back.*"

BREAKING THE NORM

Sometimes, my time becomes eclipsed,
I start to run against the circle
I welcome death to hug me
I kiss the end entirely
My mind deny to think positive neither I
I think of ending my breath,
I think of delete my name
I want to take the long leave.

ABOUT THE POEM
"*While living with great depressions, sometime it became unbearable. I decided to take my life. Life is never to give up. I changed my decision.*"

WHERE THE SUN NEVER SETS

Leisure never comes whatever it is, night or day,
A robot is working inside me undoubted restlessly!
I want an escape from the certain duties
I am chained somewhere!
The thing I say, the work I do, is never ever taken carefully,
I am silence around the world
Where the sun never sets!

ABOUT THE POEM
"The human mind gets collapsed by the thought of suicide. It becomes attacked with all types of complexities. In that situation, a person fails to decide anything. He/she feels mistreated and neglected."

APPLE VS. KNIFE

We are said to ignore that Apple,
We didn't do so,
Cutting an apple with a sharp knife sounds good
Using a knife to bleed that apple or else...
Sounds good, "Apple vs. Knife"
I decided "I vs. Knife"
I am a Human-being.

ABOUT THE POEM
Here I took the biblical reference of Adam-Eve. I tried to harm myself while I was passing bad times. At that time, I considered me as Apple and I planned to harm myself with the knife. Later on, I remembered once again that I am Human-being who can make the impossible to possible.

THAT LONGEST NIGHT

That night I failed to sleep
Of course it was not Van Gog's Starry Night!
I fought against me
I breathe death too close,
My existence was getting questioned
Is it too necessary to exist?
I answered, Long miles to go!

ABOUT THE POEM
"I had passed a pathetic night some years before. It was seemed the longest night of my life which I will never forget. As stated before, I was successful to overcome that night by remembering frost."

DARKNESS UNDER THE LAMP

I have a life full of chaos, darkness and active sprinters!
I am nothing but a lamp!

Still living with the help of light
Comes fake and vague.
Everyone sees my light from the top
No one cares about the darkness living inside me
Or I am living inside the dark?
Never put the lamp off, never loss the hope to live.
Yes, you are one of a kind.

ABOUT THE POEM
"Depression never gives a person relief. When I was suffering from great depression, I never shared my condition with others. I tried to represent myself as normal. But I was burning inside. Still I never give up."

ABOUT HASANUL
Born in Bangladesh, Hasanul is in his early 20s, and has completed his graduation in English Literature and Language, from the Jagannath University, Dhaka. As well as writing, translating and editing, he also loves to make short documentaries, and in 2019, he received the Global Impact Award from the USA. Hasanul loves to write about people, life, environment and reality, and is inspired by his father, Masudul Hoq and mother, Sirajam Monira. Hasanul dreams for a discrimination free world!
E: shoummo1971@gmail.com

Lizzie Jones's Story

Sexually abused, used and raped by her biological father, Lizzie turned to words and poetry to help her get through the horror and trauma she experienced.

"I am a very unhappy young woman, I wasn't happy as a child, or teenager, all due to being sexually abused, used and raped by my biological father, who then blackmailed me not to tell anyone what he was doing. It was painful watching others growing up, having family days out and holidays, whereas I had none of that fun; just pain, torture and suffering. My mental health issues started properly when my father eventually got exposed as a paedophile. He had his laptop stolen, and on it were 1000s of images of very young children being abused. When I learnt this, I couldn't cope; I tried to take my life, but failed. Since then all I've wanted to do is die. We lost absolutely everything when the neighbours forced us out of our home. Mum divorced him, and we were in a hostel for sometime; all we both wanted to do was to end our lives. Eventually mum and I were offered a flat, which we made our home. There was still the dark secret about what my dad had done though, and my mental health deteriorated even further. I self-harmed to get relief and see a psychiatrist and other mental health teams. And then one day, rather than talking face to face about what happened and why I self-harmed, I sat down and started to write my feelings on paper. It somehow helped. My father wasn't charged and got off, and his case in currently under appeal, so I still struggle to go anywhere, just in case I see him. Every day is like a war; it drains me of what little energy I have. My mum was amazing though, she was my rock, but she fell ill and sadly, after nine months in hospital, passed away. I've really struggled since, and have had no proper help, but I try to remain strong and turn to words and poetry to help me survive."

I'M TIRED

I'm tired of asking myself why?
I'm tired of life just passing me by.
I'm tired of struggling, when all I do is try,
I'm tired of breaking down to cry.

Tired of having no energy, and not knowing which way to go.

I'm tired of watching people laughing and having fun,

maybe because I'm scared to socially interact, and have none.
I'm tired of people making promises they can't keep,
is it really a wonder I break down and weep?

I'm tired of constantly being in so much pain, I wish it would just all go away.

I'm tired of being so sad and lonely,
and for repeatedly asking myself If Only?

And tired of not being able to do the things I once could.

I'm tired of waking up each day,
just wishing that I could feel okay.
I'm tired of faking my way through life
knowing that I'll never become a mum, or a wife.

To be perfectly honest I'm just sick and tired ... of life.

THE BEAST

I lived in a world that was full of isolation and fear. I would sit and tremble every time you were near. I could even smell you creeping up on me. But you would never stop and listen to my pitiful plea.

I was forced to do things never to be spoken about, just a little girl being forced into adulthood too soon. You took everything away from me, that one day should've been special to me. You will never have the chance to hurt me again.

I know my life will never be what I wanted it to be. My memory will be forever haunted by the vile actions of you.

All these long, hard years of living in fear has given me the strength and courage, to make a very brave decision, and talk about everything that you did to me.

THE MANY MOODS OF MY LIFE

One day I will feel happy, the next day I will feel sad.
One day I will feel really good, but the day after I feel really bad.
One day I have lots of energy, the next day I feel worn out.
One day I can be full of confidence, but the next day I'm full of

doubt.

One day I feel carefree, then the next day I will care too much.
One day I feel on top of things, but the day after I feel out of touch.
One day I can feel so brave, but day after I feel so scared.
One day I will feel ready, then suddenly unprepared.

One day I feel so proud, but suddenly full of shame; I know this isn't just me,there are so many people who feel the same. Life can be such a cruel and testing game. It's just a pity we all have to live in such misery and pain. Whilst many of us feel there's something left to gain, there are many who wish to remain the same.

BORN SAD

I'm not scared my life will end,
but so unhappy it hardly began.
In school, when all the other kids were playing,
laughing and having fun,
I'd be the one pushed away, and left alone.

Faking a smile and pretending I'm happy,
is so much easier than explaining why I'm feel bad.
I do kinda miss the days when my smile was real,
but way down deep, I was really sad.

The hardest thing I have ever done,
was to continue when my screwed up life,
when in reality all I wanted to do,
was run far away, curl up and die.

I hate the moments I've been crying,
because of who I am.
And how my life has been deeply saddened by somebody
who was supposed to be my Dad …

ABOUT LIZZIE
Lizzie has published two collections of poetry titled: *Stolen Childhood,* and *A Broken Smile.*

Prose by William Penfield (Will Pratt)

MY BROTHER'S SUICIDE

Forgive me, Dave. i should have known you better ...
We'd met for lunch just two weeks prior. dangit! i should have asked how you were: 'No, really, how are you?' Instead, i just ordered the Pastrami and then rushed back to work ... Dang ...

They said your finger-tips were badly bruised from frantically, instinctively trying to loosen the noose ... Please forgive me, Dave. I was not a good big brother. I should have saved you.

Mom called me at work. I told my boss and then just shot out of there and went to her.
I held her as we sobbed ... Dad was at the store. When i told him he yelped out like he'd been stabbed. Please instinctively forgive me, Momma and Dad.
I am not a good son. I should have saved my little brother.

Please instinctively forgive me Sue. You and Dave were good younger brother/sister: my twins!
I am not a good big brother. I should have saved your twin. I should have saved my little brother.

My precious children - Nick, Jess, and Steph, and nephews Casey, Zack, and Evan. Please instinctively forgive me. I am not a good dad or a good uncle. I should have saved your Uncle Dave. I should have saved my little brother.

Dear Sharon,
Please instinctively forgive me. I was not a good husband. I should have saved your brother-in-law. I should have saved my little brother.

Dear Heavenly Father, I confess all my sins: I am a bad son and a bad husband and a bad dad and a bad uncle and a bad big brother. I should have saved my little brother. Please instinctively forgive me and have mercy on my soul. Please don't instinctively send me down to Sheol. I pray in your name.

Please.

ABOUT WILL

Will's writing 'career' can be traced to May, 1969 when he completed 40 Haiku for a 5th grade Social Studies assignment. He earned the grade, 'H' (Of High Quality), and the comment, 'Excellent'. In spring of 1976, Colorado's Bicentennial, he entered a high-school Essay Contest, 'What It Means To Be A Coloradan'. He was awarded 2nd Place. That same spring, his poem *Into Your Eyes* was accepted for publication in *The National High School Poetry Press*. For his final project in an alternative 'Senior Seminar' class, he self-published a short collection of his poems titled *Voices From A Mirrored Pond*. Finishing high school, his poem *Desert Dream* was published August 7, 1977 in the Poetry Forum of *The Denver Post*. Also, around that time, Will won 1st Place for his *Ode to a Peak* in the 'We Write' poetry contest. Finally, in December of 1977, his *Ode to a Peak* was again published in the Poetry Forum of *The Denver Post*. After having graduated from Arvada West High School, his poem *Seasons* was published in the Arvada West *Claw* yearbook in the spring of 1978. Thereafter, college, family, and career overtook him, and the only writing he did was technical - Standard Operating Procedures (SOPs) for Environmental chemical analyses - save an Application Review for Petroleum in the June 15, 1989 edition of *Analytical Chemistry*. In Winter 1996, *Inklings* published Will's Book Review of the Welsh poet, Dylan Thomas' *Portrait Of The Artist As A Young Dog*. Will wrote his provocative poem, *Apologies to Mr. Einstein,* which was promptly published in the 2020 issue of *Colorado Country Life*. Recently, his poem *Prayer to the Anasazi* was published in the Winter 2022 anthology of *Our Changing Earth* (Vol. 2), and was selected as 'The Poet's Featured Poem' on January 25, 2023.

E: jwpratt21958@gmail.com

Poetry by Gargi Saha

DEPRESSION

I find no joy of living
No fun in jokes
No happiness in success
No grief in miseries
I have become static
And, one with the diurnal course of life
I am just existing
Not living with all senses
I like to withdraw
Myself from the daily chores of life
I hesitate to giggle loudly
Weep deeply
For I am being lost
In the forests on non entity
Hence I am submerging myself in the ocean of loud silence
Don't ever try to contact me.

I FEAR TO

I fear to stay alive
Alone
To see my only daughter
Always quarrelling with my one
And only son in law

I fear to stay alive
To see domestic violence
Prevailing in higher echelons
The elites struggling in the mundane, materialist deserts
Of competitions, conflicts and cold wars

I fear to stay alive
In a single room, partitioned house
Of doubts, uncertainties, phobias
Shattered by the weird mentalities
The haunting egos of supremacy
Eccentricism, maladjustments, arrogance
I wish to sublime and sink
In the valleys of serenity and engulfing benevolence, altruism

Where minds will be without fear
Where minds can soar to heights of imagination
To attain sublimity of the soul
Where there is love, there is respect
Where there is friendship, there is accommodation
Where there is politeness, there is honour
Where there is caring, there is hope
Let me fly unnoticed, avidly
In a priceless territory of unmatched duality.

ABOUT GARGI
Gargi lives in India. She is a creative writer, and has published two poem books, *The Muse in My Salad Days*, and *Letters to Him*. She recentlyr eceived the Rabindranath Tagore Memorial Award, and the Independence Day Award for poetry. She is a member of various poetry groups on Facebook, and presently she edits several scientific research papers.
E: gargi.paik@gmail.com

Interview with Alshaad Kara

Tell me more about the mental health problems you have had and their history.
We all face depression in our lives, there is no shame admitting it because we all felt low and lost at a certain point in time, and I did too.

Can you identify how and when it first started?
I would say it started when I was around 15 years-old, as I was getting bullied on a daily basis.

But was there a specific life event which propelled it further?
Yes, the worse happened when I was constantly sexually harassed in 2020. Yes! Men also face such situations. No one believes us, or it's simply puffery. I felt completely shattered because I never asked for it, nor I consented to it. What was worse was I did not know who to talk to, who would believe me and - honestly speaking - it is still hard to face it again and again because, as men, we do not have the platform to really be vulnerable or expose ourselves as survivors. It brings you to a state of overthinking, anxiety, stress and depression. There is a sense of sadness that prevents you from feeling safe.

How did you feel?
I felt very lonely and in pain. I felt like my own dignity is ripped off your soul. It's not because you are handsome, or a boy that consent shouldn't be asked. Even if it's a constant "no," it is still a "no!" I didn't want to feel like I felt. I was compelled to, and the world around me was to blame. The environment was so unsettling that I felt unworthy and very tired of being judged, when I didn't do anything wrong.

How did you cope at the time?
I tried to keep my mental health strong by putting up a shield. I can say that it does really help to mask that pain quite easily, unfortunately.

Are you still facing sexual harassment or any sort of uncomfortable situations?
How I wished I could say otherwise and say it was just a bad nightmare! I know it will still happen with the kind of individuals, mentality, and the thoughts that people have. It definitely affects oneself but I will not let those unpleasant events affect my whole life. I choose my life's story despite unforeseen circumstances.

What processes do you use to help and support you through the difficult times?
Meditation helps to calm down my anxiety. To monitor the depression inside me, I do try not to burn out.

Is there anything or anyone in your life that has helped you through?
Yes, my closest friends. Surround yourself with mature people, or people who have been through the same situations who will listen, guide you, and help you out.

Was there a catalyst in your recovery?
Yes, since I decided to take the right direction - that is doing what would be best to improve my life, it helped me to build my self esteem and confidence. It really changed my perspective in life by living life fully, as if there is no tomorrow.

What help and advice can you give others going through the same challenges?
Save yourself, because you are your own character of your story. It's not easy - I know - but there are always moments awaiting you further on in life that are worth it. Realise to not care about what people think of you; love yourself like you would love someone else.

What do you think should be done as a global society regarding mental health and sexual harassment?
The first initial step is to have the courage to voice out, and if we, as a global society, do not let our people express themselves with their truths, then we live in a society which is condemned to regression. It is mandatory for people of all ages to be provided with the necessary platforms, guidance on the procedures and legislations and what to do in moments where one's mental health is affected or if they are faced with any uncomfortable situations. Victim blaming, or secondary victimisation, should not be acceptable, and there should be a penalty for it. No situation is too small; we should realise that victim support and follow-ups are the options that will help to make our survivors stronger. Actions should be taken against those who dare to harass, or break one's mental health too, without leniency, since it has caused irrevocable damages to the one suffering.

When did you start using poetry to help you?
In 2019, that's when I started to do so, having both losted a close one, and had a heartbreak the preceding year. Since I write from my heart, it has always been a helping-hand when I am filled up with

emotions, good or bad. Feelings are the heart's desire to express, and this is what I do with poetry. Music helps too.

Where do you like to write and when?
I don't have a specific place or time. It just happens.

Have you had any poetry published?
My poetry has been published in many countries including Australia, USA, France, India, Pakistan and Canada. The greatest thing is to be able to put my country, Mauritius, on a global stage, and this is my greatest achievement in my heart!

How could other people benefit from writing poetry?
If you feel lonely, or you do not know whom to talk to, writing poetry can help to alleviate your pain and push you to write wonders.

INSTANT SOLITUDE

The confusion of the mind,
Is the trajectory that one takes,
To end the tragedy.

No one speaks of it bluntly.
Yet it is hard as spilling a truth,
Without being rebuked
For one's vulnerability.

The danger that one
Faces in loneliness
Is the dust
That pile up
Without any hope
For a different tomorrow.

Giving up
Is the trajectory that one takes,
To finally end the tragedy.

ABOUT THE POEM
Loneliness is the obscurity that keeps you awake. This is what I felt at times in my depressive state wanting to terminate my own suffering.

INTENSE REGRET

If is the word that will always be my regret.
There is not a day that I do not have those flashbacks.
It takes only one moment to crash
One whole lifetime.

The words exchanged are daunting,
With no fear to keep haunting
The memories I behold.

With the self harm you inflicted,
Will always be the scars
That scarf the surface of my soul.

The past remains unchanged,
With the present affected
By those previous memoirs ...

That shall forever follow me
From behind.

ABOUT THE POEM
"This piece is an experienced feeling of having lost someone to suicide, when I went through that same route myself some time back. It is a scorching feeling that hits you at heart, because every time I think of that time, it reminds me eventually of that departed soul as well."

BROKEN CONFIDENCE

I gave my full self to you,
That I lost myself.

The full autonomy I gave,
Was to serve your grace,

Which you manipulated,
And,
Played
For your own content.

The humiliation I faced,
Had no words to fill in.

You shattered my soul,
That I no choice,
To remove myself,
From your threatening torture.

So, I am self-destructing myself
In hopes of not having to meet you again.

ABOUT THE POEM
"I hope this piece can help someone out there not to go through the self-destructive part of giving oneself blindly, like I did. Love should not harm you in any way."

EMPTY EMOTIONS

Dear All,

My culpability of holding everything together,
Fails miserably.
All the time.

I tried,
Alas, I failed.

With a profound regret,
I tried to let go of everything,
For a last time,
To attain peace,
In my deep mind of pain.

It felt comforting to not suffer anymore,
But I survived!

My culpability of showing myself together,
Fails miserably.
In that shameful time.

I tried,
Alas, now am a survivor
Facing the wrath of my own suicide.

ABOUT THE POEM
"This piece highlights my own aftermath of having experienced suicide at first-hand."

SHAKEN

I can still feel the knife near my wrist,
The desperation has come
To complete
My own sunset.

The real truth
Is the hideout of the pain
That keeps resurfacing silently,
Without anyone knowing

That you are suffocating in that suffering,
With a silver lining
That makes you peel the truth away,

In times that one needs to fake,
In front of the world,
In front of the mirror.

ABOUT THE POEM
"This autobiographical piece reflects that you have to hide your pain for the sake of society when they, in the first place, make so many boundaries to make you suffer."

ABOUT ALSHAAD
Alshaad is a Mauritian poet who writes in English, French and Italian. His latest poems were published in two anthologies: *Love Letters in Poetic Verse* and *The Talk, Delicate Conversations by Families of Color; an anthology of essays, letters, and poetry on the topic of Racism*. He has also had work published in two magazines, *100subtexts (Issue 7),* and *Prodigy Magazine* (February, 2023), and one journal, *Orion's Beau Winter 2023: A Love Worth Losing*. He has won a Diplôme d'Honneur at the 'concours littéraire des Jeux Floraux des Pyrénées 2023'. Additionally, more of his poetry work can be found in *The Suburban Review* (Issue #25: Juice); *Love Letters to Poe, Volume 2: Houses of Usher; parABnormal Magazine* (September 2022); *20.35 Africa: An Anthology of Contemporary Poetry Vol. V; Italian Poems; Région Centrale Numéro 5; All Voices Heard Volume 1; Tidings 2022; The Wonders of Winter, Coeur de plumes Numéro 6;* and *The FEEEL Magazine* (14th digital issue, Dec 2022).
Instagram: @alshaad_kara
Instagram: @teamalshaadkara

Poetry by Bhuwan Thapaliya

THE SLIT INSIDE MY HEART

The slit inside my heart grew wider
as the cavity in the nicotine-stained
teeth of my grandfather
and the feeling that it was time for me to go
to allow more space for them to breathe came back again
during last year's World Economic Forum at Davos.

From the second day of the forum itself, I was scared.
I was scared of the dawn. I was scared of dusk.
I was scared of anything in between.
I was as scared as a sacrificial goat shivering in fright
 as it awaits its turn on death row
in the blood-stained Bhagawati temple
nearby my village home in the lap of the Himalayas.

My days were entirely brittle as the instant noodles I despise
and everything appeared gray to me including the bright Davos Sun.
I looked up at myself in the mirror and shyly smiled.
I looked okay, aside from the stubborn wrinkles beneath my eyes.
But I was anxious, shaking, and dismayed all the time.

Lost in confusion, I had lost my direction.
I walked to the window and opened it
to kiss the ground below with my heart.

Suddenly, a large blue face of my ancestral tutelary deity
danced before my eyes, and the image of my poet friend
Amar Akash's little messiah puppy
running around in the backstreet of Kathmandu
saving lives came flashing before my eyes.

I closed the window and had my dinner early.
I lay awoke in my bed, and counted the hours
 before I could greet the dawn again
and have a safe flight back home.
On the adjacent sofa, my dreams and hope
 slept with their arms around each other.

ABOUT THE POEM
"An economist friend of mine, a depression patient, almost committed

suicide at the World Economic Forum, in Davos, Switzerland. Fortunately - according to him - he was saved by two things; his ancestral deity, and his friend's little puppy. Amazing isn't it? But we are so lucky to have him around us now, and we are encouraging him and motivating him to be strong all the time, and live his life. Now he is doing fine, though he is under medication. I want to share this poem with the world because it's the survivor's tale."

ABOUT BHUWAN
Bhuwan is a poet writing in English from Kathmandu, Nepal. He works as an economist. He is the author of four poetry collections, and his work has been extensively published internationally.
E: nepalipoet@yahoo.com

Poetry by Qurat ul Ain

DEATH OF HOPE

The cries are still loud and shout
And the eyes were bruised.
The Dark clouds of loneliness,
Spreading the veil slowly.
The city of Love and
The threads of peace
Now lost!
The mornings now,
Are dressed with pitiless nights.
The light of togetherness
has blurred and dimmed.
Fair winds show anxiety
to the breaths.
What's it?
A mere death?
A just loss?
I wonder! How life takes all hope along
How the river of longing flows by the cold chest.
You're Gone! But the shadows still fall upon the eyes.
You bury the life,
They lost hope and joy
Oh, Mother!
Your lost smile was tucked and plucked.
By and by life ends,
But the live eyes are sealed for long.
Life is taken for once,
But the Ephialtes never end!

Poetry by Andrija Radulović

SWALLOW
Translated by Nikola Djukić

No one dived like that
From the bridge

People used to come
From afar
To see
His swallow
To catch
His dive

One time
He didn't come out

He embraced the rock
Below the bridge
As his
First love

ABOUT ANDRIJA
Andrija is a poet, essayist, editor of several literary journals. He studied History at the University of Montenegro, and graduated from the Teacher Education Faculty at the University of Novi Sad. He has published the following books of poetry: *View From the Bridge, Sign in the Sand, Midnight on the Don, The Burning Rib, Word from the South* (a bilingual selection of short poems in Russian and Serbian), *Angel in the Wheat, Snowy Alphabet, The Burning Rib* (in Bulgarian and Romanian), *White Bee of Walt Whitman, If I Could Cry as a Vineyard, General and the Swallow*. His poems have been published in English, Russian, Italian, Spanish, French, Greek, Bulgarian, Romanian, Hungarian, Arabic, Macedonian, Danish, Czech, Slovak, Polish, Hebrew and Ukrainian, and he has received the following awards: Gramota of the Literary Museum of Bulgaria, International NOSSIDE award (UNESCO), Aninoasa (Romania), "Božidar Vuković Podgoričanin", "Kočić's Quill", "Marko Miljanov", "Balcanica" (award from the Festival of Balkan poets in Romania), "Boris Kornilov" (Saint Petersburg) and others.
E: nikoladjuk@t-com.me

Poetry by Caila Espiritu

LIFELINES

     Faint streaks from a time
My red pen oozed tingling, hot
         Sensations—seep in

ABOUT THE POEM
"'Lifelines' is a Haiku that evokes the fleeting sensation of self-inflicted cuts, and the harmful cycle caused by an intense desire to feel. It is structured in a way which resembles the physical marks that will always remain on one's skin."

ABOUT CAILA
Caila was born in the Philippines, raised in Hong Kong, and is a recent Contemporary English Studies graduate. She often writes poetry and song lyrics. While mostly she writes privately, she has recently begun publishing and submitting them for contests. Verbalizing her thoughts as a quiet and reserved person can be challenging, but she finds her way around it through these creative outlets. Writing aside, she also enjoys dancing and photography. As her journey into the real world begins, she aims to: 1) further expand her creative potential, 2) find a personal style that accurately reflects her ideas, and 3) hopefully make a name for herself in the industry. She cherishes every opportunity given to showcase her craft, and she looks forward to what the world has to offer.
Instagram: @arcai.vz
Medium: @caila.espiritu
YouTube: @arcaivz

Poetry by Cass Erickson

WHY?

Why?
Why now?
Why couldn't they have waited one more day, one more night?
Why didn't we see it coming? Or perhaps we did
       but the relationship didn't warrant
              this kind of inquiry
Why didn't someone step in and try?
Why did they choose an early exit?
What made it imperative?
Was it inherited?
Was it generational trauma?
Why wasn't there one person at the funeral of 500 people
       who could have gotten through
              just one
Why were they so hell-bent?
Why were they so full of self-doubt
       and yet certain about this?
At what point did they turn the corner
       toward oblivion—
Why didn't they get out of their own way?
What of their faith?
A faint glimmer of hope
is better than none
Cass Erickson, Why?, page 2, continue stanza
       even as a deceit—
              it would have sufficed
What about all the other times they hung in there?
Thinking maybe something good might happen
       eventually
Who or what made them want to do this?
Why didn't they leave a note?
Why did they leave a note?
Why didn't they fight back?
Run away?
Get on a plane and go somewhere—
What were the stories they were telling themselves?
That weren't true
Why didn't they call a friend?
Why didn't they have a friend to call?
Why does everyone judge them as if they were of sound mind?

Why?
Why?
Why?
We will always ask Why?
Why doesn't time make it any better?
Why?
Because it could have been averted ...

ABOUT THE POEM
"I wrote this poem as a witnessing to the loss of three friends by suicide. Each person was very different, as were their circumstances, but they chose the same exit. Each time it happened, I always wrote about it, sometimes at great length. Writing is how I process my life, expressing my feelings and thoughts, as I try to make sense of the human condition. Suicide is heart-rending subject matter but sadly, very much a reality."

ABOUT CASS
Cass is a poet, an award-winning playwright, and short-story writer currently residing in Minnesota, USA. Her poem, T*he Duel at Our Doorstep*, appeared in The Poet magazine's *Our Changing Earth Anthology, vol. 2. Alpha Dogs,* a ten-minute play, was produced off-Broadway by Love Creek Productions in New York, and had a staged reading at Chicago Dramatists. The play was invited for a staged reading at the Last Frontier (Edward Albee) Theatre Conference in Valdez, Alaska. *Insomnia*, a ten-minute play, was produced by Flying Leap Players in Grand Marais, Minnesota. *Every Shiny Object* had a reading in the Ten-Minute Play Festival at the Playwrights' Center in Minneapolis, Minnesota. *Zigs and Zags*, a one-minute memoir written for radio, was a finalist in *Brevity: The Podcast of a Journal of Concise Literary Nonfiction*. *Forks of Ivy*, a full length play, was a finalist in Trustus Theatre's Playwrights' Festival in Columbia, South Carolina. Sponsored by Lex-Ham Community Theatre in Saint Paul, Minnesota, Cass directed a staged reading of *Forks of Ivy* at the Lowry Lab Theatre. *Ennui,* a monologue, was published in *Mother/Daughter Monologues: Volume 4: Urgent Maturity,* by the International Centre for Women Playwrights (ICWP) Press. Her short story, *Diamonds in the Sky*, was a finalist in the E.L. Doctorow short story contest sponsored by the Writers Workshop in Asheville, North Carolina. Cass is a member of the Playwrights' Center in Minneapolis, Minnesota, and the International Centre for Women Playwrights.
LinkedIn: @casserickson

Poetry by Chris Butler

TALKING THEM OUT OF SUICIDE

I want to die,
but I always
talk them out
of suicide,

why?

There's no inside,
only nature's
blistering outsides
of painful plains,
why I can complain,

but give me death!
One last breath!

And an end.

Previously published by the literary journal In *Between Hangovers* in 2016 and will be featured in Chris Butler's upcoming next collection of poetry.

ABOUT THE POEM
"The poem is about an individual struggling with their own thoughts of self-harm or suicide, trying desperately to save the love of the loved one who also is experiencing the same crisis."

KNIGHT AND DEATH

When the white Knight
reaches the rocky beach
at the end of his flat earth,
Death
challenges the unknown soldier
at the end of his last crusade
to a game of high stakes chess.

Glistening steal armor versus a black cloak,
the game begins with pieces arranged
with endless possibilities, but only one
inevitability…the beheading of god.

Each move is followed by doubt,
sending another soldier to a casualty
as Death casually orders the murder
of the front line of frightened white pawns.

The Knight follows the horizontal
and vertical positioning by the bishops,
neighing with doubt as each shoed
hoof clicks and clatters across the board.

The stampedes charge across the board,
but not in time to save the queen,
the Knight's one love, as her cries were left
unheard under the silent reply of crashed waves.

Death allows vengeful rage to lead to mistakes,
as the Knight unleashes upon the black army to jestingly
prolong the attacking warrior's last show of defiance
as he reached the last row in the rear of his opponent ...

"Check ..."

Death could not envision his army parting,
the battled field by the raining blitzkrieg of the blood
of an inferior foe, unleashing a tornado of swords

The inevitability still exists that Death
wins the war every time, but there's
still a chance for victory in everyday battles.

 "... mate".

Previously published in the chapbook *DOOMER* published by Ethel Press.

ANGELS' WINGS

Angels
in three piece
suits

don't need
to spread their
wings

to fly
into the
sky,

away
from the peace
of clouds

paved with concrete,

as the
rest of us
are left

with skyscrapers' skeletal remains.

Previously featured in the poetry collection *Montage of Madness* published by Scars Publications.

ABOUT THE POEM
"Dedicated to those jumpers who lost their lives on the morning of September 11th, 2001, at the former World Trade Center in New York City."

SUICIDE SONG

When there is nothing left
and I've chewed my last chalky antidepressant,
my eyes glance to shiny synthetic disks.

I open the plastic case and the port on my stereo
to place the plastic wax on its outlined tray, allowing
the lackadaisical laser to scan through the tracks.

A disfigured finger presses the seek button
to skip towards my sacred sad song,
then is preset on a continuous loop for eternity.

Sometimes I find myself thinking
That these skinny wrists need slitting,
But I must be kidding …

The symphony of bittersweet cacophony bursts
in distorted waves from the speakers.

Puffing packs of cigarettes
Is cheaper than a box of bullets,
Yet it's better not to know it ...

The discord of the singer's vocal chords express
endless verses of angst-ridden lyrics.

Flying kites at night,
Under the bright white lighting strikes,
Is prayer my life takes flight ...

The bass bumps persistently against my ear drums,
mirroring the rhythm of my fading heart.

It's just my style
To fit the tragic profile
Of a downward spiral.

Previously published in the chapbook *Antimatter* by Scars Publications.

ABOUT THE POEM
"*A classical poetic form that I wrote and subsequently published in my college poetry writing class, dedicated to a friend of mine who decided to end his own life to the soundtrack of the dying soul.*"

EVERYTHING IS WRITTEN IN PENCIL

The eraser
chafes
the paper,

tainting
blank canvasses
with the graphite
ghosts of my
mistakes,

until my skin
sloughs
off dead
tree cells

and brushes the
consequences of

thoughtless actions
away.

Previously featured in the chapbook *Artsy Fartsy* published by Alternating Current Press.

ABOUT THE POEM
"The poem is a representation of how, even though the writer may erase their mistakes on the page with a pencil, the ghostly visage of their errors stick with them as apparitions against the paper."

HEMINGWAY'S WAY

Hemingway's way
can be found on
an inland island,
where an unlovely
loner skips individual
sandy granules over
evaporating oceans,
yearning to be kissed
by glass lips protruding
for breath from the top
of a brown paper dress,
before performing
oral pleasure
upon a loaded
twelve-gauge
pump-action
shotgun,
just for fun.

Previously published in the chapbook *Antimatter* by Scars Publications.

ABOUT THE POEM
"Dedicated to one of the modern world's most famous figures and writers who sadly met their untimely end by their own hand."

ABOUT CHRIS
Based in Connecticut, USA, Chris was once labelled as "the next rising star of the underground poetry scene" by three publishers at the age of 23. At the age of 37, he has published over 500 poems and multiple short stories, academic and creative essays, news articles and book reviews. His acclaimed *Poems of Pain* series of poetry collections includes three books and seven chapbooks, including *DOOMER* (Ethel Press), *Artsy Fartsy* (Alternating

Current/Propaganda Press, with 12 selected poems from the chapbook also published in The Camel Saloon's *Books on Blog* series), *BUMMER, The War of Art, Emo, Antimatter* (published as e-books by Scars Publications), and *Neurotica, Montage of Madness and Down Syndrome* (Scars Publications). He also co-wrote a book of poetry with Randall K. Rogers entitled *Dead Beats* (Dakota Publishing Company). Butler's poetry has garnered six awards and honours from different publishers. Five of his poems have also been read live, or recorded by publishers and other artists and posted to YouTube, including *Morning Wood, Wonderland* and *When a Pregnant Woman Reads the Surgeon General's Warning.* He is also the co-editor of *The Beatnik Cowboy* literary journal.
W: www.beatnikcowboy.com

Poetry by Bernie Martin

MISSING PERSON

Struggling silently along a snow covered street.
Thoughts stuck in the past with people he has to meet.
Riverside lunches would help secure a deal.
A past he's left behind, a wound no time can heal.
Tonight he'll recount his tales but to no-one's ears.
Family and friends are left to live with their fears.
Once fine clothes are now parcelled up in purple bags.
River Avon opens its arms to this man now in tatty rags.
Disappeared with no goodbye, no note, no reason why.

THE NIGHTMARE

Still everything is redolent of her there,
living as we are the worst possible nightmare.
Sleep is something we have to learn to live without.
Can't abide staying in but don't want to go out.
Remembering a smile, the obsession with hair,
living as we are the worst possible nightmare.
Trying to tell ourselves she's not already dead,
regretting arguments and the things we all said.
An interested look becomes a vacant stare,
living as we are the worst possible nightmare.
Sounds that for us will never be the same again,
happiness experienced only now and then
and all the time desperate to remember when

ABOUT THE POEMS
"Both these poems are based on personal experience of people I knew."

ABOUT BERNIE
Bernie lives in England. He has been writing for 25 years or so; mainly poetry, but also short stories and a novel.
E: har4vey@aol.com

Poetry by Syed Ahrar Ali

POEM 1

I picked it up in an instance
Words I never knew, formed
The choices, unexplored were born
The lives of a summer font

I showed up at your party
Looking to feel the enclaves
Losing my heart in the stares
Feeling unworthy in my grave

To the hearts that craved
The lies that had enslaved
I felt it like a lump in my throat
Travelling to the gut, it strayed

You showed up to my parade
Breaking like a promise said
Feeling all the heartaches
From promises of yesterdays

I turn away, leaving the frays
A mind's behest, of flight
Leaving the stars, I believed
Running away to exhaustion

My mind strayed again, afloat
In the river, I found myself
On an afloat body, I climbed
Giving in temptation, to drown

Swimming away from the corpse
Of my past I had held strong
Till the hands gave out
Blood dribbling from wrists

Suddenly eyes opened, a meadow
Believing it to be my destination
Heartaches still linger by
Of words that I denied

Ran in that meadow, I screamed
Of rights and wrongs, I still bleed
Serenity in my mind as it eased
I finally woke up from my dream

POEM 2

I wake up often at night
Salt streaming from my eyes
Blood clotting on the thighs
With the end not in sight
I try to reclaim the prize
Removing the scabs of the night
Letting it trickle once again
To let myself feel the pain
To rid myself of the stain
A blemish which the oceans drain

POEM 3

My palms are stained red
Yet they appear blue to me
Maybe it shows me my nature
Of the coldness I try to fathom

The hands trickle red
Still only the blue appears
Colour blind? Or is it my fear?
My questions grow in a haze

Red and blue, a combination true
Alive we are red, I do not crave
The heartaches and the sad proses
In blue death is where I find solace

POEM 4

Hoping to erase you from my mind
I always find myself in a bind

Of the throes of heart that cried
The love I had all this time

Wishing to pull that strand of time
Hoping you'll once again be mine

I kill the cells of my arm in a line
The blood trickling, flowing as fine wine

My heart jolts to the memory I admired
Of a love that I never felt was mine

I try to kill myself all this time
I torture the heart, till it cries

ABOUT THE POEMS
"While I wrote the poems, it was hard for me to talk about what I was going through at the time, maybe the poems better explain what it was than any other words could."

ABOUT SYED
Syed lives in Pakistan. He was born into a family of writers and poets, so it was not long before he took up the mantle. He finds inspiration to write from the abstractness of life, with most of his work focused on trying to find a universe hidden in a single word. A decade back, Syed found his love for English poetry, and since then it was impossible to hold him back. Writing is like breathing for him, which is why he writes for a living, and then when he is done with that, he writes for himself. With that kind of love for the language, words seem to flow like water, which he often combines with his love for journaling.
Instagram: @unrelentlessmusings

Poetry by Edvin Sarrimo

PANIC-ATTACK

Tight grip on the fork. Pungent smoky odour rising from the empty glass. Obsessive thoughts on mutilated bodies and screams of burning monks. I don't believe in God, but his absence is a knife to my throat.

ZOLOFT

I used to be a window, now just a bricked-up smile. But I swing from snare to snare and laugh at the hangmen down there. Comfortable to have no worries, but the price is tall: The sky quotidian as a bus shelter, my mood flat like a chipboard.

ZOMBIE

I can't bear to think anymore. Just want to listen to voices I agree with or don't care about. Just eat pills out of the hand of life.

FOOTPRINTS ON THE OCEAN FLOOR

The stars are an indifferent audience. They couldn't care less about the show. I spit on them and leave the stage. All that's left: A few footprints on the ocean floor.

ABOUT THE POEMS
"I live in Paris, France. I'm going through a deep depression at the moment, and the poems touch upon the emotional effects of panic, anxiety and suicidal thoughts, as well as the positive and negative sides of medication. I hope readers can either relate to, or just enjoy the poetic language."

Poetry by Dr. Koyal Biswas

I AM ON MY WAY, BROTHER!

He wasted no time
in rushing his way out
while
the tiny message
rang an unanticipated alarm
he knew
for sure
he meant 'no harm.'

He drove
like
the mad gush of a cloud burst
in the heart of the city traffic,
praying all the way
to the heavenly father
to help him
reach out for his safety.

Once, twice, thrice and many more times
the door bell rang in vain:
Killing the silence of the vicinity
the young man stood in pain.
His breathe screamed louder
and
throat dried in fear,
his heart beat grew faster
when
he found no one at the door there.

What happened next
Was a report in the newspaper
Read the headline,
"I am on my way, brother."
The suicide note
Followed:
"The targets of the company
have taken away my peace;
life holds no meaning
with pretence of success
and

my EMI reminders reached me
before a birthday wish.
Tired with all deadlines
now I take this leap:
I am on my way, brother
to a never-ending holiday break."

ABOUT THE POEM
"This incident was witnessed by my counselee. I met this young man, whose mother is a close friend of mine. She complained her only son, aged around 32, has shut himself inside his room. I pondered over the news and came to know that the young man's friend committed suicide. Although he rushed to save him but in vain. After having witnessed suicide of his friend, the young man was terrified, shaken and sank into depression. When I met him, we did not waste any time and I handed him over to a team of specialists. Today, he is living a normal life and have gathered all the courage to face life once again."

ABOUT KOYAL
Koyal is a Senior Assistant Professor in Hindi language and literature, presently working in Mount Carmel College, Bangalore, India. She is also heading the Department of Hindi. She is a certified Counsellor and a Life Skills Coach. Her publications include more than 30 research papers, more than 200 poems in Hindi, and about 100 in English. She has also authored and edited over dozen books. Her poems largely include man and nature, essence of true love, and the intervention of science in humanity. Her first English collection of poems will be published very soon.
E: koyalbiswas@gmail.com

Poetry by Mariana Mcdonald

UNVARNISHED

He drank it like a soda fountain drink
to quench a thirst, chockablock
with ice, a straw, and bubbles.

It was meant for stubborn floors faded
by old varnish, acid crystals aimed to
blanch the surface, make things new.

It went from his troubled lips into
his oesophagus, as if he'd swallowed
fire in some circus side show act.

In his gut were fireworks, explosions.
Organs stunned by the display
uttered hemorrhagic gasps.

Body fluids pooled all about him.
Someone finally heard the moans,
called an ambulance to take his body.

The coroner declared it was time for prayers,
not questions. Parents claimed his heart
gave out, saying he was dead because he died.

Siblings searched for clues and found the puzzle pieces:
an open jar, scrawled notes, paled planks, revealing
it was suicide that bleached him of all life.

ABOUT THE POEM
"'Unvarnished' is about my brother's suicide. My brother was born with a birth defect that made his life extremely difficult. When a surgery that promised to improve everything didn't work out as he'd hoped (with no counseling services offered), he fell into profound despair and took his life by poisoning himself, ingesting varnish remover. It was an excruciating death. To add to the pain and torment of it, my parents refused to accept that he'd taken his own life, and the coroner utilized religious platitudes to cover it up. This was many years ago, when the stigma of suicide was very much worse than it is today."

ABOUT MARIANA

Mariana is a poet, writer, scientist, and activist, and lives in Georgia, USA. Mariana's work has appeared in numerous publications, including poetry in *Crab Orchard Review, Lunch Ticket, The New Verse News, Les Femmes Folles, Clerestory, The Poet, We Are Antifa, Poetry in Flight/Poesía en Vuelo, Fables of the Eco-future*, and *Anthology of Southern Poets: Georgia,* among others; and fiction in *About Place Journal, So to Speak*, and *Cobalt*. She trained with Al Gore in 2019, and joined the international Climate Reality Leadership Corps. She was named a Black Earth Institute Scholar Advisor and Fellow for 2022-2025. As a young adult, Mariana lost her brother to suicide; his death has impacted her whole life.

E: marianamcd@yahoo.com

Poetry by Christopher Martin

MERRIE ENGLAND
For My Mother, Ann

We'd pull a wishbone together over the table
with our pinkies; two thin, wet bones joined at a point,
or one little fork, separated with a wish.

Whatever happened to Merrie England?

Who was pulling you apart on the kitchen floor?
A breath blowing out a breath, a flickering name,
keeping us in the dark?

Because of you I never wanted for anything.

I could have wished we'd revolved a while longer
round that table. Like the spools of the Patsy Cline tape
you played whilst cooking, cleaning, washing …

"Crazy for thinking that my love could hold you"
Played to death.

Two thin, wet bones joined at a point, one small fork
in the road; I was left holding the shorter pink clavicle
and you wanted to end your life.

LUNG SOUNDS , BEACH

Long after kids and seagulls
                Competed for the highest note

And someone shouted out
                To a distant, passing boat

And the calls of the owners
                Dogs pretended not to hear

And the shrieks of tourists
                Avoiding waves on the pier

And the bells rang out

        From St. George's church

After the coast guard had
        Called off the night search

Water sluices through the silence
        Of nothing anyone could say

The only sound remaining
        Longsands beach, Mother's day

Is the crossing of the boatmans palm
        Moon passed from tongue to hand—

The unbroken waves of an outbreath
        Relieved from sand to foreign sand.

ALTERATIONS

When you'd pick your legs they'd weep like the eyes
of pale Aspens. The boys at school didn't hide their
disgust from me one time, I'm sorry I was embarrassed.
Your seamstress fingers deft repairing little holes
in the universe; or making them.

Through threaded throats blue tits embroidered
broken song, when you undid the last stitch of your beauty.
Pinpointed pills chalked seams for the ripper, and the world
came away; dark cloth gathered round the feet of the Singer,
left under the ghost light at Camden Alterations.

"OURS NOT TO REASON WHY, OURS BUT TO DO OR DIE"
After Alfred Lord Tennyson

You said, and held true to it.
A belief we didn't share, and yet

Phantom hooks swing
Through the undulating waves
Of a white flag,

The mark of death sinks
Like a stone, rolled over the open wound

Of the obedient mouth,

Silently awaiting corporeal communion.

The charge of the darkness
Through your blue veins
Into the valley of death.

I am without reply
And never reasoned why,
But what little can I do?
And *how much* can I die?

AN CUAN A TUATH

Living by the shoulder of the North East coast is An Cuan a Tuath—
North Sea. Held by the earth in its cold, cupped hands, moving like
a blue tongue in the mute river mouths of colder lands, reciting a litany
of flux. It lives here by me now, poised, as then in the photo
by the soft, bare shoulders of the child I was on Longsands Beach.
The photo you carried in your purse at all times. I wonder
was it the last thing you saw before turning out the light? How tight
was your grip? How steady your hand? Did you raise your lips to my face
as you lowered me into the sand?

"please never forget me as the years go by"

The sand envelope sheathing the photo and a note, a litany of grief,
lowered into the grip of words like the disembodied, pressed leaf. Memory
begins with our mother, she is that to which we first return; to warm,
cupped hands, never spilling a drop, never dropping a stitch, held out
like St. Kevin's unconditional nest, cradling the delicate bones of faith.
Those hands captured this small, sea bleached window, out from which
I'm looking back at you; An Cuan a Tuath by my side, it's litany suspended
in blue. The tide will find its way in, to sand in photos, to words held in sand,
to the dune formed from the delicate, hollow bones, crushed in the hand.

ABOUT THE POEMS
"These poems relate to both my mother's suicide, and to other separate experiences. There has been a history of suicide in my family; my mother - who was my only immediate relative other than a distant father - took her own life when I was 21 years of age. The poems, which are a result of the healing process of long-term trauma, manifested organically and unwilled, and when I first began to put them down on paper it came as quite a surprise. In a way they demanded to be written; many details from the past surfaced that had been forgotten or possibly suppressed. The way they emerged left me in no doubt of the healing power of poetry and of their importance - at least to me. It was, and still, is a powerful experience being involved with them; deep, latent wounds needed release and found their way up and out through the creative act. I have come to know that poetry is a glorious expression of health, sanity, and of love. Early in 2022, in a change to my original intentions, I came to the conclusion that my debut collection, should be centred around my experiences with suicide and the resulting healing process. I needed to honour both my Mother and my own journey. It felt inevitable. I hope that in some way they will be of benefit to anyone navigating the same difficult and lonely terrain."

ABOUT CHRISTOPHER
Christopher is a poet and Buddhist living by the mouth of the Tyne on the north east coast of England. His work has featured in various publications, anthologies and events including: Sam Lee and the Nest Collectives Singing With Nightingales *Homecoming*, Linda France and New Writing Norths 'collective sound poem for the beginning of the world *Dawn Chorus*, highly commended in Folklore Poetry's 'Poems for Trees' competition, runner up in The Black Cat Poetry Press 'Sea' competition, and shortlisted for their 'Tree' competition, Sunday Mornings At The River Poetry Diary 2023, *Poetry for Ukraine* and *Our Changing Eart*h anthologies, Black Bough Poetry's *Tutankhamun* Edition, The Wee Sparrow Poetry Press *Still We Rise* revolution poems free digital zine and shortlisted by Mike Curry Photography for *Fleeting Reflections 2*, and featured several times in *Ekphrastic Review*. His debut collection is due 2024.
Instagram: @martintimations
Twitter: @Martintimation1

Poetry by Finola Scott

SOOTHE

Black sweatshirt sleeve
slips,
filigree scars
flash silver.
Veins pulse hot below
fragile flesh. .

In next room TV
chatters, talk is small.
Mum
pleased you're home
safe, away from the bullies.
In princess-pink room after school
away from taunts and tripping, you
practice.

Edge near, nearer

Tender skin sliced,
tiny rows scored scarlet.
Each slash screams silent.
Despair given voice.

This time.

A version published in the *Poetry Shed* (2015)

ABOUT FINOLA
Based in Glasgow, Finola is a proud grandmother. Her poems are published widely.
E: finolascott@yahoo.com
FB: @Finola Scott Poems

Poetry by F. E. Scanlon

I WILL NEVER ASK WHY

Suicide no more ends Life than Death ends War.
Politicians sign Peace Treaties but individuals don't opt-out on hybrid self-warfare.
Soldiers fight wars of endless Liberation while prisoners of self-annihilation.
The End of Watch is only the end of a beginning.

The Upper Room awaits the crescent of salvation.
Shuffling sand knows well that once a war begins it never ends.
The past is prologue.
The past is never past.

Easy to forget is so very important to remember.
You came to me in a dream last night for the first time.
You awoke me to your presence.
There might have been a braying donkey to herald your Arrival.

The dead of night lit your path.
Strut static interrupts the currency of your Being but not for long.
Your last email to me referencing a day-to-day matter counseled: "Why get involved?".

Indeed I'll never give up on You.
You didn't give up on Yourself.
You exited your earthly Self.
For a destination unknown.

I can squash all the grapes in Life's vineyard and I will never know why your vitality desiccated.
I can run a zillion ultra marathons and I will never know your starting point.
I can sail every marooned sunset from here to somewhere and I will never know why your vessel tipped.
I can somersault every movement on the scales but I'll never know why you walked off the dance floor, alone.

Visit whenever and wherever the Spirit moves you.

I will never ask why.

ABOUT F. E. SCANLON

F. E. Scanlon, is an Attorney, born and raised Manhattan, New York. A *Jazzie* since age four, whose by-line feature articles and film reviews have appeared in *Newsday, Irish Echo, Brooklyn Daily Eagle, Times Ledger Newsgroup* and the *Queens Gazette*. Her poetry appears in a number of magazines and literary journals.

OTHER TITLES:

OUT NOW

SUICIDE (Vol.1)
A collection of poetry and short prose from writers around the world on the themes of suicide and self-harm.

First published 2019, Updated December, 2022
ISBN: 9781091029347

To order a copy, go to: www.PoetryforMentalHealth.org

FORTHCOMING

ADDICTION
A collection of poetry, short prose, interviews and personal stories from around the world on the theme of addiction.
June 2023

PTSD
A collection of poetry, short prose, interviews and personal stories from around the world on the theme of PTSD.
August 2023

To contribute to these titles, or to sponsor them, go to:

www.PoetryforMentalHealth.org

SUICIDE Vol.1
A collection of poetry and short prose from writers around the world on the themes of suicide and self-harm.

First published 2019, Updated December 2022

ISBN: 9781091029347
Available as a larger format 6 x 9 inch (15.24 x 22.86 cm) paperback and Kindle.

175 pages, 48 contributors, 20 countries

It is undeniable that putting thoughts, feelings and emotions into words, on paper, either with poetry or in a short story format, can be both therapeutic and an incredibly effective method of self-help and healing. In this brave and uncompromising collection - which also includes a number of personal interviews - forty-eight writers and poets in countries around the world including: *Australia, Bangladesh, Bahrain, Benin, Brazil, England, Germany, India, Ireland, Italy, Japan, Malawi, Malta, New Zealand, Nigeria, Pakistan, Scotland, South Africa, Switzerland* and *the USA*, creatively explore the themes of suicide and self-harm, either from their own personal perspectives and experiences, or from the experiences of friends, family and people close by. An anthology on these subjects is undoubtedly thought-provoking and emotional, but also positive and uplifting too as, for many, putting their feelings into words has set many on the road to creativity, healing and ultimately recovery.

W: www.poetryformentalhealth.org/suicide